THE CAPE OF GOOD HOPE
G.S.M. MEDAL ROLL

AUTHOR'S NOTES:

This Roll has been prepared from Microfilm housed in Africana Museum, Johannesburg – microfilm of the original applications, mostly on a specially printed form, C.F. Form No. 253, which form was to be a list of "Officers, Non-Commissioned Officers and Men, now serving in the above Corps who are entitled to the Cape of Good Hope General Service Medal." The Roll was, when completed, to be forwarded, in duplicate, to the President of the Medal Board, Defence Department, Cape Town, through the prescribed channel.

Eight headings on the form called for the following details:

(1)   Present Rank and Number (if any).
(2)   Surname (in alphabetical order).
(3)   Christian Name (in full).
(4)   Rank and Number at the time Medal was earned.
(5)   Corps at the time Medal was earned.

Campaign for which Medal was earned.

(6)   Basutoland 1880-1.
(7)   Transkei 1880-1, including Tembuland and East Griqualand.
(8)   Bechuanaland 1896-7.

The application form for the medal called for the Surnames to be listed in alphabetical order, and the hand-written Medal Roll was then prepared – with the surnames listed in order of the alphabet but in no way in strict alphabetical order. Whilst this method of recording has made the tracing of a medal most convenient, from a collector's point of view, this is unsatisfactory, for the number of medals to a particular Regiment or Unit cannot be determined without further considerable research.

A Roll has now been presented by Units – this form of presentation has called for many hours of writing, checking and re-checking and, whilst the Author believes this to be an accurate record, a gremlin may have crept in.

The original returns were invariably hand-written – in particular those submitted by the Cape Town Highlanders were in beautiful copperplate scrip – a work of art – those, however, submitted by the Duke of Edinburghs Own Volunteer Rifles, for the Basutoland Campaign, were just the opposite, and most difficult to read.

Twenty-three names are recorded as having received all three Clasps to the medal – full details are given herein.

The Roll also records ten names as having received the Medal WITHOUT A CLASP. Of the ten it appears that seven, could have been the victims of careless recording, but the other three, viz:-

   (1)   Nurse G.A. Rogers - No Unit
   (2)   Pte. P.A. Williams - C.M.R.
   (3)   L/Sgt. J. Wilson - C.M.R.

show undeniable evidence that their medals were issued without a Clasp.

The rank of Private and Trooper was most loosely used, for example, the names recorded under:-

    Richmond Burghers

    Somerset East Burghers

    Willoughby's Horse

where both Troopers and Privates took part in the same actions. As I am unable to check whether, or not, there were both these ranks in many of the Units, for sake of convenience, some headings thus appear as Tpr/Pte.

The uninitiated may wonder why anyone should spend many hours in preparing and printing a Roll of this nature. Medal Collecting and Military History Research calls for frequent reference to Official Records- records which invariably lie many miles away, either in Cape Town or Pretoria, but mostly in London from whence information is generally efficiently available. The acquiring of this information, however, calls for correspondence and delays. A Roll, of course, gives a permanent record of all that is known regarding the issue of the medal.

Medal Collecting today has become big business, and high prices are being paid for rare medals - a purchaser wishes to know that his medal is a genuine untampered acquisition - his only proof is the Medal Roll, so it was with this thought in mind that the Roll was printed.

This Roll contains 5.156 individual names. All the awards were in silver - to the white and the non-white combatants. The Medal, designed by G.W. de Saulles, was awarded by the Cape Government in terms of Government Notice No.841 of 1900 - (at the height of the South African War 1899-1902).

This work is a record of the names of those who received the Medal - in no way is there any indication of the number of Officers and Men who took part in these three Campaigns - some 16 to 17 years apart - and it is more than possible that some of the Units then present are not even mentioned herein, as there were no claimants for the Medal. I have in my researches found reference to the following, who do not figure in the Roll:-

    Albany and Beaufort Rangers

    Barkly Special Burghers

    Captain Poole's

    Cummings Fingoes

    East London Cavalry

    Engcobo Native Levy

    Eva's Hottentots

    Langkloof Volunteers

    Mount Fletcher Native Contg.

    Mounted Rifle Club Mafeking No. XII

    New England Volunteers

    Royal Durban Rifles

    Spriggs Own Border Rifle Vols.

    Sterkspruit Volunteers

    Umschlanga Native Levy

    Vaalhoek Mounted Vol. Cavalry

    Van Linsingens Horse

Xesibes Native Levies

Young's Runners.

It is more than likely that few who served in Basutoland or the Transkei in 1880-1, particularly in the small Units, (Websters Rovers had a life of but 32 days with a strength of 31) were still serving, some 19 years later, when the Queen approved of this Medal - no doubt many were dead and many more were then in action against the Boers - a large number, perhaps, had never even heard of the Medal, or was it too much trouble to first of all obtain "the prescribed form" and then apply for the Medal?

On the 9th July, 1900, the Commissioner of Police District 1 (see copy of letter herein) listed 1.048 names of the Police who had been engaged in the Bechuanaland Campaign and who qualified for the Medal - it is interesting to see the number of Medals ultimately issued - here follows a breakdown of those figures:

DETAILS OF NAMES SUBMITTED		DETAILS OF MEDALS ISSUED	
Majors	1	Majors	Nil
Captains	9	Captains	4
Lt.	27	Lt.	18
W.O.S.	1	W.O.S.	1
Sgts.	39	Sgts.	25
Cpl.	35	Cpl.	28
L/Cpl.	70	L/Cpl.	59
Pte.	385	Pte.	248
Sp.Police	69	Sp.Police	14
Sp.Native Police	78	Sp.Native Police	Nil
Native Detec.	119	Native Detec.	49
Native Troops	215	Native Troops	131
	1.048		578

Just more than half of the Cape Police D.1. received the Medal, this is hardly surprising, in view of the conditions of the award. NOT ONE of the 78 Special Native Police obtained a Medal and only 49 of the 119 Native Detectives did so. Despite the fact that 180 Medals were awarded to the non-White members of the Cape Police D.1. and other non-White combatants also received the Medal (Vide Willowvale Native Contingent), I know of but two of the Medals to non-Whites - one to No. 1039 Native Private Patela and of another in the hands of a prominent Cape Town collector - what could have happened to the rest?

With a total issue of 5.252 Medals (being 5.156 individuals plus 96 duplicates/triplicates) this Medal, covering three Campaigns, must surely be considered a scarce medal - especially as so many of the Units listed herein have but ONE medal awarded. So too, the medal to Nurse G.A. Rogers or the 23 medals, with all three Clasps, are in the rare class.

THE CAPE OF GOOD HOPE GOVERNMENT GAZETTE,
TUESDAY, DECEMBER 4, 1900.

GOVERNMENT NOTICE No. 841 - 1900

PRIME MINISTER'S OFFICE, CAPE TOWN, CAPE OF GOOD HOPE,
3rd DECEMBER, 1900.

His, Excellency, the Governor, with the advice of the Executive Council, has been pleased to approve of the following Regulations regarding the issue of the Cape of Good Hope General Service Medal

SYDNEY COWPER
Secretary to the Prime Minister.

CAPE OF GOOD HOPE
GENERAL SERVICE MEDAL

(1). Her Majesty the Queen has been graciously pleased to approve of a medal being granted to the officers, non-commissioned officers, and men of the Colonial Forces who were engaged on active service during the following campaigns, viz:

    (a)   Basutoland   1880-81

    (b)   Transkei   1880-81 (including Tembuland and Griqualand East.)

    (c)   Bechuanaland 1896 - 97

(2). The medal will be issued to all survivors who, during any of the campaigns specified in paragraph (1) performed under orders from competent authority:-

    (a)   Active service in the field

    (b)   Served as Guards at any point where an attack was expected or

    (c)   Were detailed for some specific or special military service or duty.

(3). Clasps inscribed:

Basutoland, Transkei and Bechuanaland, respectively, will be granted to those entitled to the medal.

(4). No medal or clasp will be granted to any member of the Colonial Forces who deserted or was dismissed for misconduct.

(5.) Officers Commanding existing Permanent or Volunteer Corps will prepare nominal rolls, in duplicate, on the prescribed forms, of all officers and men still serving in their respective corps who are entitled to the medal.

When complete, these rolls must be forwarded, in the case of the Permanent Forces, direct, and in the case of the Volunteer Force, through the Commandant of Volunteers or Officers Commanding Colonial Artillery, to the President of the Medal Board, Defence Department, Cape Town.

Claimants for the medal who are no longer members of any Permanent or Volunteer Corps of the Colony should submit their applications direct to the President of the Medal Board on the prescribed form.

AUTHOR'S NOTES:

(1) The Medal 1.42. inches (3.61 cms.) in diameter, with a darkish-blue ribbon, and a sand coloured stripe down the centre, from a straight suspender, has the bust of Victoria and the legend VICTORIA REGINA ET IMPERATRIX" - the reverse being the Arms of the Cape Colony with motto "Spes Bona".

(2) No mention is made that the Medal could be issued WITHOUT A CLASP, yet I have quoted herein reference to certain Medals without Clasps.

(3) The Medal was issued in Silver only, to all claimants - both White and Non-White.

(4) Those killed in action or who died on service received NO award.

NO CLASPS   The following received no Clasp to their Medals:-

1. Pte. S.R. Daniel   C.M.R.
2. Cpl. S.K.C. Daly   Papkuil Rifles
3. Col.Sgt. V. Ewers   Stutterheim L. 1 Vol.
4. Sgt. W. Haig   Dukes
5. Pte. H.H. Norton   C.M.R.
6. Nurse G.A. Rogers   No Unit

7. Sp.Policeman A.A.Smith Cape Police D. 1
8. Pte. E.G. Smith   Dukes
9. Sgt. J. Wilson   C.M.R.
10. Pte.P.A. Williams   C.M.R.

DUPLICATED ISSUES OF MEDAL:

I have on record that 94 Medals were duplicated.

TRIPLICATED ISSUES OF MEDAL:

Pte. J. Laaks of the Kaffrarian Rifles had Medals sent to him on 1.7.1902, 21.7.1902 and 30.3.1909.

Cpl. Bugler T. Wiley of Prince Alfreds Volunteer Guards had Medals sent to him on 5.7.1902, 15.7.1905 and 17.6.1907.

CAPE OF GOOD HOPE GENERAL SERVICE MEDAL - 3 CLASPS

RECORD NO.	NAME	RANK	CORPS	DATE SENT TO A.G.	DATE SENT OUT	Roll	
1851	Bobbins, J.	Driver	P.A.O.C.V. Arty	1. 5.01	9. 6.02	Roll	17
2928	Chiappini, A.L.	Capt.	C.M. Yeo	16. 7.02	15.10.02		48
2627	Coombs, E.C.A.	Gnr.	C.F.A.	26.12.01	31. 7.02		39
1537	Curran, J.	Pte.	Nesbitts L.H.	27. 3.01	13. 6.02		12
457	Dye, E.H.	Sgt.	Cape Police D. 1	6. 3.01	5. 6.02		9
475	Gillwald, F.W.H.	Lt.	Cape Police D. 1	6. 3.01	18. 6.02		9
1403	Hartley (V.C.), E.B.	Surg.Maj.	C.M.R.	20. 2.01	24. 5.02		7
3293	Hutcheons, A.N.M.	Capt.	Wodehouse B.Rov.	20. 8.02	11.11.02		50
818	Lust, J.	Pte.	Nesbitts L.H.	23. 1.01	18. 9.03		3
1851	McArthur, R.	Sapper	Cape T.Vol.Eng.	1. 5.01	9. 6.02		17
951	McDonald, H.	Sgt.	Nesbitts, L.H.	10. 4.01	25. 6.02		14
2020	McGuire, E.	Tpr.	C.M. Yeo	29. 5.01	12. 7.02		21
797	McLean, R.	Capt.	Buffalo Vol.	27. 3.01	25. 6.02		12
475	Marsh, C.S.	Sgt.M.	Landreys H.	13. 3.01	18. 6.02		10
1537	Nielsen, C.	Pvt.	Nesbitts L.H.	27. 3.01	13. 6.02		12
2448	Peakman, T.C.	Sgt.	C.F.A.	2.10.01	24. 6.02		33
1317	Pillans, R.	Lt.	Dukes	17.10.01	26. 5.02		15
3472	Quine, R.	Pte.	Cape Town Rifles	10. 9.02	23. 7.03		51
1851	Rodwell, T.	L/C	Dukes	1. 5.01	9. 6.02		17
1537	Strutt, S.	Pvt.	Nesbitts L.H.	27. 3.01	13. 6.02		12
11/1327	Turner, A.	Pte.	Ushers Cont.	?	13. 9.06		65
475	White, A.J.	Sgt.	C.M.R.	20. 3.01	18. 6.02		11
3093	Willemite, W.D.	Pte.	C.T. Rangers	21. 1.03	20. 6.03		56

Note: The headings to the columns are those of the Medal Roll.

CLASPS TO THE MEDAL:

Basutoland	1.589
Transkei	562
Bechuanaland	2.483
Basutoland/Transkei	490
Basutoland/Bechuanaland	77
Transkei/Bechuanaland	18
Three Bar Medals	23
No Bar Medals	10
	5.252

TWO CLASP MEDALS:

About 11% of the 5.252 Awards had two Clasps - my count shows a total of   585

In view of this small number, a two Clasp Medal, must surely fall, in the "scarce" category.

The TRANSKEI/BECHUANALAND

Combination shows but   18
whilst the
BASUTOLAND/BECHUANALAND
Combination   77

The hand-written Medal Roll (now sadly dilapidated) started off with neat accurate detail, but by 1905 the recording was careless and the handwriting, in many instances, had become almost childlike.

The periods covered by the bars were as follows:-

<u>Basutoland</u>   13th September, 1880, to 25th April, 1881.

<u>Transkei</u>   13th September, 1880, to 15th May, 1881.

<u>Bechuanaland</u>   24th December, 1896, to 30th July, 1897.

Medals with the two Clasps Basutoland and Transkei, generally have the Transkei Clasp nearest the Medal - this Roll shows the Clasps, as called for on the original application form C.F. Form No. 253, which firstly lists Basutoland, then Transkei and Bechuanaland. The medal roll lists Basutoland first.

Should anyone wish to copy this Roll, for any purpose, it will be necessary to obtain my written permission to do so.

7th April, 1975.
Reprinted.
26th September, 1979

D.R. FORSYTH
265 Harley Road,
Blackheath, Johannesburg. 2001
Tel. 678-1072

ACKNOWLEDGEMENTS AND THANKS TO:

Africana Museum, Johannesburg - Dr. Anna Smith for photographic copy of the original returns.

Dr. S. Kaplan for supplementing information.

Mr. G. Stewart for information.

Mr. Ian Uys for assistance.

Captain S. Webster for assistance.

Mrs. Martie Henning for outstanding typing.

The Department of Defence, Chief of Staff, Pretoria for providing The Medal Rolls for checking purposes - in particular WO. 1. H.L. Engelbrecht S.M.

The Head of Government Archives, Union Buildings, Pretoria, for his consent that enabled the Department of Defence to release the Rolls to the Author.

The Department of Military Intelligence also gave its concurrence and co-operation.

ABALONDOLOZI REGIMENT

Rank	Name	Ba	Tr	Be
Capt.	Adendorff A.R.		X	
	Bonner J.W.	X	X	
	Cranney W.H.	X		
	Dallamore J.M.	X	X	
	Hulley T.F.	X		
	James A.F.	X	X	
	Rouquette H.E.	X	X	
	Scott G.R.		X	
	Sloley H.C.		X	
	Stafford W.H.	X		
	Usher J.	X	X	
	Wright G.D.		X	
Lt.	Banger W.R.	X	X	
	Booth W.	X	X	
	Castle C.J.		X	
	Chaniir H.	X		
	Goldsworthy A.E.	X	X	
	Hornsby H.L.		X	
	Seymour H.	X	X	
	Tucker W^m.	X	X	
Pte.	Chaplin W.H.		X	

ADELAIDE MOUNTED INFANTRY

Also listed as Adelaide Volunteers and Adelaide Mounted In. Volunt.

Rank	Name	Ba	Tr	Be
Sgt.	Hollis J.P.	X	X	
	Mills R.	X		
	Pitt J.		X	
Cpl.	Hollamby T.	X	X	
	Long R.	X	X	
Tpr.	Andrews W.	X	X	
	Bishop W.J.	X		
	Chipps T.W.		X	
	Midgley G.F.	X	X	
	Midgley J.H.	X	X	
	Russon I.C.	X		
	Sparks R.T.		X	
	Walker J.B.		X	

ALBANY RANGERS.

Rank	Name	Ba	Tr	Be
Capt.	Attwell W.T.J.	X		
Qms.	Impey W.G.	X		
Sgt.	Wilmot W.J.	X		

ALBANY RANGERS Contd.

Rank	Name	Ba	Tr	Be
Cpl.	Chiddy T.J.	X		
	Latham C.A.	X		
Tpr.	Baines J.B.	X		
Pte.	Berrington S.T.	X		
Tpr.	Clack H.R.	X	X	
	Clack T.	X		
	Clack W.T.	X		
	Collings R.V.	X		
	Emslie J.C.	X		X
	Farley W.H.	X		
	Hewson G.	X		
	Hewson J.	X		
	Lanham T.E.	X		X
	Mitten A.E.	X		
Bugler	Powell E.J.	X		
Tpr.	Rippon V.	X		
	Wilmot G.A.	X		
	Wright J.J.		X	
Pte.	Shaw B.	X		

ALBERT BURGHERS.

Rank	Name	Ba	Tr	Be
Cpl.	Coetzee J.N.	X		
Pte.	Londt S.	X		
	Snyman J.H.	X	X	
	Wilhelm G.F.	X		

ALEXANDRIA BURGHERS.

Also listed as Alexandria Contingent

Rank	Name	Ba	Tr	Be
Lt/Adj.	Newcombe J.P.		X	
Sgt.	Deacon F.C.		X	
	Mynhardt J.M.		X	
	Oosthuizen G.I.		X	
	Saunders C.W.		X	
	Swartz C.J.		X	
Bugler.	Bruton C.M.		X	
Tpr./Pte.	Berry J.O.		X	
	Bosman C.P.		X	
	Bosman D.W.		X	
	Bosman J.J.T.		X	
	Carroll M.		X	
	Dunsterville E.W.		X	
	Maritz H.F.		X	

ALIWAL NORTH CONTINGENT.

		Ba	Tr	Be
Cpl.	Guthrie A.	X	X	

ALIWAL NORTH VOLUNTEERS

		Ba	Tr	Be
Pte.	Goddard E.	X	X	
	Howard C.H.	X		
	Ramsbottom E.H.	X		

AMATEMBU REGIMENT.

		Ba	Tr	Be
Capt.	Dalziel R.W.		X	
	Davis J.P.	X	X	
	Holder J.H.		X	
Lt.	Hallaway C.K.		X	
	Kelly J.A.C.		X	

ARMY ORDNANCE CORPS.

		Ba	Tr	Be
Sgt./Arm.	Bullock E.D.			X

BACA CONTINGENT.

		Ba	Tr	Be
Commandant.	Leary W.P.		X	
Capt.	Garner W.H.		X	
	Maynard C.M.		X	
Lt.	Armstrong F.W.	X	X	
	Dallamore A.W.	X	X	
	Hulley E.		X	
	Wardle J.		X	

BAKER'S HORSE.

		Ba	Tr	Be
Surgeon.	Allen R.R.		X	
	Johnston D.W.		X	
Lt.	Hughes-Chamberlain R.E.	X	X	
	Molyneux W.H.A.	X	X	
	Prendergast T.A.	X	X	
RSM.	Griffin G.	X	X	
Sgt./Maj.	Gray W.	X		
Farr. Sgt.	O'Keefe D.	X	X	

BAKER'S HORSE/ Contd.

		Ba	Tr	Be
Sgt.	Bradley A.T.	X		
	Brock J.J.		X	
	Collins G.P.		X	
	Lungoge C.G.	X	X	
	Middelborough H.J.	X		
	Sargeant E.		X	
	Slatter W.		X	
Cpl.	Bodmer A.O.	X	X	
	Crowsen J.T.		X	
	Power H.S.	X	X	
	Von Berg A.		X	
L/C.	Allen J.		X	
Tpr.	Atkinson W.N.	X	X	
	Bunce W.G.		X	
	Chapman J.C.	X		
	Cochrane R.		X	
	Crowsen W.	X		
	Dare N.	X		
	Gilbert T.		X	
	Gilbert W.F.		X	
	Harold R.		X	
	Hislop H.	X	X	
	Holt J.	X	X	
	Jessop J.R.	X	X	
	Kelly J.J.	X	X	
	Lemcke W.		X	
	Lewis S.J.	X	X	
	Lister J.B.		X	
	Lord F.		X	
	Manderson E.R.	X	X	
	Mansel F.R.		X	
	Maroney P.	X	X	
	Payne A.H.	X	X	
	Prentice J.		X	
	Rogers G.	X	X	
	Rose S.		X	
	Scribbins A.		X	
	Sidney A.P.	X		
	Smith J.H.		X	
	Spring H.D.			X
	Stephenson D.	X		
	Steward T.		X	
	Stocks T.		X	
	Stuart W.	X	X	
	Taylor H.		X	
	Thompson W.R.	X	X	
	Thring J.L.		X	
	Tomlinson W.		X	
	Turner J.	X	X	
	Waffron J.T.	X	X	
	Warbrick W.H.		X	
	Watson R.		X	X
	Wilson E.C.H.		X	
	Woodroffe A.C.	X	X	

	Clasps		
	Ba	Tr	Be
BARKLEYS NATIVE CONTINGENT.			
Sgt. Cassidy L.M.	X		
BARKLY VOLUNTEERS.			
Capt. Halse H.E.		X	
BASUTOLAND MOUNTED POLICE.			
Also listed as Basuto Special Police / Basuto Police.			
Lt./Col. Schermbrucker T.	X		
Capt. Couper G.J.	X		
Liefeldt J.B.	X		
Inspector. Schwarzkopf H.	X		
Sgt. Masin I.	X		
BASUTO NATIVE CONTINGENT.			
Also listed as Basuto Native Levy. / Basuto Levy.			
Commandant. Leifeldt M.W.	X		
Capt. Glazbrook C.E.H.	X		
Hall W.H.	X		
Peacocke N.F.	X	X	
Welby R.E.	X		
Lt. Hart F.	X		
Qms. Hanneford J.F.	X		
BEAUFORT RANGERS.			
Capt. Richards J.	X	X	
Lt. Harley W.	X		
Niland B.		X	
Tpr. Hacking W.J.	X	X	
Windell B.F.	X	X	

	Clasps		
	Ba	Tr	Be
BEAUFORT WEST BURGHERS			
O/Sgt. Roper J.F.R.		X	
Cpl. Clark J.	X	X	
Holmes J.		X	
Tpr. Peters J.T.		X	
BEAUFORT WEST VOLUNTEER RIFLES - Also listed as Beaufort West Rifles			
Capt. Barber C.M.	X		X
Fripp H.E.		X	
Sgt. Rice E.W.		X	
Solomon R.E.		X	
Cpl. Roskelly R.		X	
Pte./Tpr. Blyth J.A.		X	
Davis W.J.	X	X	
Fowlkes G.		X	
Morgan A.W.		X	
Townsend J.W.		X	
Williams C.		X	
BECHUANALAND FIELD FORCE BECH. S. POLICE - Also listed as BECHUANA F.F.			
Chaplain to Force King P.J.F.			X
Surgeon Lt. Fenboulet J.P.			X
Vet Surgeon. Tomlinson G.N.			X
Paymaster. Brade A.D.			X
Guide. Chapman E.H.			X
Interpreter. Brown S.C.			X
Asst. Storekeeper. Mallett W.E.			X
Tpr. Chichester A.J.			X
Incorrectly named BULAWAYO F.F.			
Pte. Smith A.H.			X

		Clasps		
		Ba	Tr	Be

DESPATCH RIDER NATIVE CONT.

		Ba	Tr	Be
	Leach W.A.			X
No Rank	Smyth J.			X

BEDFORD BURGHERS.

		Ba	Tr	Be
Lt.	Grassie P.		X	
	Trollip A.J.A.		X	
Tpr.	Absalon J.L.		X	
	Clift W.H.		X	
	Drake J.W.L.		X	
	Fitchet J.W.	X	X	
	Hinton F.		X	
	O'Brien W.		X	
	Peacock W.C.		X	
	Richards C.H.		X	
	Richards H.		X	
	Williams W.		X	

BORDER POLICE.

		Ba	Tr	Be
Tpr.	Leane W.J.		X	

BREDASDORP BURGHERS.

		Ba	Tr	Be
Capt.	Thom W.C.T.	X	X	
Pte.	Thorpe W.Z. deB.		X	
	van Brakel J.J.		X	

BUFFALO MOUNTED VOLUNTEERS.
Also listed as BUFFALO VOL. BUFFALO M. VOL. BUFFALO VOL. RIFLES.

		Ba	Tr	Be
Capt.	Ludwig H.A.		X	
	Maclean R.	X	X	X
	Selzer C.	X		
Lt.	Rissling A.		X	
	Rogers T.S.	X		
	Rustenburg	X	X	
Sgt./Maj.	Warren W.	X		
Sgt.	Hynes J.	X	X	
	Schnepel P.		X	
Cpl.	Bearschank W.B.	X		
	Sergel H.	X	X	
Tpr./Pte.	Cornill S.G.	X	X	
	Deutschmann C.H.E.	X		
	Diemer F.	X	X	

BUFFALO MOUNTED VOLUNTEERS/Contd.

		Ba	Tr	Be
Tpr./Pte.	Donald A.E.	X		
	Ford W.H.	X	X	
	Francis C.	X	X	
	Fraser J.	X	X	
	Frietag F.F.	X		
	Hopf A.	X		
	Jefferies A.J.	X	X	
	Klose H.	X		
	Kretschmann C.A.	X		
	Lederle F.	X	X	
	Pachonick F.	X	X	
	Pachonick J.	X		
	Paddock M.J.	X	X	
	Pohlmann J.F.W.	X	X	
	Rusteburg A.		X	
	Schafli M.W.		X	
	Stern W.	X	X	
	Stewart A.	X		
	Tiltman C.	X		
	Ziehl R.F.W.		X	X

BUFFALO RANGERS – Also listed as BUFF. MTD. RANGERS.

		Ba	Tr	Be
Pte.	Cederblad C.W.	X	X	
	Fellows W.	X		
	Ford W.H.	X		
	Fraser J.	X	X	

BULLERS MOUNTED.

		Ba	Tr	Be
Pte.	O'Leary D.	X	X	

BURGHERSDORP BURGHER F
Also listed as BURGHERS^P VOLS.

		Ba	Tr	Be
Tpr./Pte.	Brandt W.J.	X		
	Marran J.C.	X		

CALEDON BURGHERS.

		Ba	Tr	Be
Lt.	Veales J.	X		
Pte.	Geldenhuis Z.J.W.		X	

CAPE FIELD ARTILLERY.

Rank	Name	Ba	Tr	Be
Major.	Giles G.E.	X	X	
Lt.	Heyman H.M.	X		
Sgt./Maj.	Kenyon T.	X		
Sgt.	Barnett E.A.	X		
	Conway J.M.H.	X	X	
	Peakman T.C.	X	X	X
	Robson J.H.D.	X		
	Spencer J.W.	X		
Cpl.	Morley W.H.	X	X	
Bombardier.	Davis T.	X	X	
1c Trumpeter.	Pike W.	X		X
Pte./Gunner.	Adams J.	X	X	
	Blyth H.M.	X		
	Brown H.H.	X		
	Chapman F.	X	X	
	Coombs E.C.A.	X	X	X
	Cuniff M.		X	
	de Villiers J.A.	X		
	Graves W.H.		X	
	Hobbes R.D.	X		
	Holey P.	X	X	
	Moore T.H.	X	X	
	Mitchell C.	X		
	Parkinson F.C.	X	X	
	Pearce E.W.	X		
	Ramsey F.A.	X		
	Reardon T.	X		X
	Rich A.	X		
	Rimell F.	X		
	Rogan C.	X		
	Snowball J.	X		
	Tafford F.W.	X	X	
	Winchcombe J.	X		
	Wright W.T.	X		

CAPE INFANTRY.

Rank	Name	Ba	Tr	Be
Pte.	Coghlan T.	X	X	

CAPE MEDICAL STAFF CORPS. Also listed as CAPE M.S. CORPS. MED. STAFF.

Rank	Name	Ba	Tr	Be
Civil Surgeon.	Green A.P.	X		
Sgt./Maj.	Dexter W.H.			X
Sgt.	Fiford H.W.			X
	Fynn H.C.K.			X
	Hatton J.			X
	Morris W.			X
No. 2 Sgt.	Smith J.			X
Cpl.	Clack T.G.			X
	Smithers G.E.			X
L/Cpl.	Jenkins C.H.			X
	Smith C.C.			X
Bugler.	Owen W.			X
Pte.	Callaghan B.			X
	Engle H.			X
	Jeary J.G.			X
	Kirsten J.W.			X
	Lance W.			X
	Leuw L.			X
	Livingstone A.			X
	Munzel L.G.			X
	O'Shea J.			X
	Radley R.J.			X
	Rousseau W.P.			X
	Spears J.			X
	Volkwyn J.S.			X

CAPE MOUNTED RIFLEMEN.

Rank	Name	Ba	Tr	Be
Colonel.	Bayley Z.S.	X		
	Carrington F.	X		

CAPE MOUNTED RIFLEMEN Contd.

		Clasps		
		Ba	Tr	Be
Major.	Bourne J.W.	X		
Surgeon Major.				
	Hartley E.B. (V.C.)	X	X	X
	Smith J.A.J.	X		
Surgeon Lt.	Knapp G.H.			X
Vet.Capt.	Dawkins T.B.S.	X	X	
Capt.	Blaine A.E.B.	X		
	Cochrane J.P.	X		
	Garnett G.	X		
	Grant J.M. (Also Hon.Maj.)	X		
	Hatton E.F.	X		
	Maclean J.K.	X		
	McCarter W.A.	X		
	Montagu H.S.M.	X		
	Staunton F.H.P. de L.	X	X	
	Waring J.C.N.	X	X	
	Woon H.V.	X		X
Lt.	Best J.	X		
	Birbeck T.C.	X		
	Brownlow W.	X		
	Carstensen A.	X		
	Goldsworthy C.L.J.	X		
	Graves G.G.E.	X		
	Leighton B.B.M.		X	
	Lukin H.T.	X		X
	Roy J.E.G.			X
	Stewart R.B.	X		
	Sutherland E.	X	X	
	Turner W.J.St.J.	X		
	Ward G.D.			X
	West C.S.	X	X	
R.S.M.	Cantwell R.F.	X		
	Collier C.O.	X	X	
Sgt./Major.	Bodle W.	X		
	Court J.M.	X		
	Edwards J.	X		
	Fiveash J.A.	X		
	Glover A.J.	X		
	Joplin F.B.	X		
	Mc Millan C.C.	X		
	Ryan T.	X		
	Schumann F.	X		
	Stier W.	X		

CAPE MOUNTED RIFLEMEN Contd.

		Clasps		
		Ba	Tr	Be
Sgt.	Abbott C.E.	X		
	Barlow C.F.	X		
	Bell B.W.			X
	Bolton F.E.			X
	Bolton W.J.			X
	Bolze A.L.	X		X
	Bowers D.A.H.			X
	Brown J.			X
1st Class Sgt.				
	Burgess G.	X		
	Butt J.	X		
	Cahill M.			X
Sgt.	Campbell H.G.F.			X
	Carstensen H.	X		
	Catchpole E.H.			X
	Church J.H.	X		
	Cole W.	X		
	Cooley A.H.	X		
	Court N.E.	X		X
	Craigie A.	X		
	Crewe C.P.	X		
	Davis J.R.	X		
	Dethier E.M.			X
	Dunn J. Mc D.	X		
	Dwyer J.C.	X		
	Edwards H.			X
	Forsbrook C.S.			X
	Fradgley E.	X		
	Gibbin W.	X		
	Graham H.D.	X		
	Hallifax G.	X		
	Hannan W.H.	X		X
	Hill J.	X		
	Hobson A.W.	X		
	Holden W.			X
	Jacob P.L.F.	X		
	Kennan T.P.	X		
	Lamb W.C.	X		
	Lindsay A.	X		
	Lock E.	X		
	Lord W.	X	X	
	Mc Cabe W	X		
	Mc Callum R.J.	X		
	Meade H.	X		
	Mumford W.H.	X		
	Neville H.M.	X	X	
Farr.Sgt.	Norton E.	X		
	Norton M.	X		
	Ockenden O.G.	X		
	Palmer F.A.	X	X	
	Parr D.B.	X		
	Payne G.T.	X		
	Pearce J.	X		

CAPE MOUNTED RIFLEMEN Contd.

Rank	Name	Ba	Tr	Be
Sgt.	Phillips W.H.B.	X		
	Prichett G.H.	X	X	
	Reynolds R.J.	X		
	Richardson W.	X		
Lt.Sgt.	Roberts G.P.			X
	Sarril P.H.	X		X
	Schenk W.M.	X		X
	Scott H.T.	X		X
	Scott W.S.	X		X
	Smith H.A.	X		
	Straw W.P.	X		
	Style S.R.	X		X
	Taplin E.A.	X		
	Taplin H.F.B.	X		
	Thomas J.V.	X		
	Tothill F.T.	X		
	West E.J.	X		
	White A.J.	X	X	X
	Wilson J.	No Clasps		
	Worrall S.	X		
Cpl.	Allman A.H.	X		
	Barnes E.G.F.	X		
	Bartlett F.W.	X		
	Biden A.H.	X		
	Bodkin J.M.	X		
	Burne N.H.M.			X
	Campbell L.			X
	Collier R.	X		
	Conran L.C.			X
	Court O.H.			X
	Cowley A.J.			X
	Eaton T.A.			X
	Eeekin W.S.	X	X	
	Evans A.R.			X
	Eve H.	X		
	Every W.A.	X		
	Fillmore M.	X		
	Freeman W.E.			X
	Gardiner A.E.			X
	Givens G.N.	X		
	Gobey J.J.	X		
	Gould S.F.	X		
	Grasskopff L.A.	X		
	Harbor W.A.	X		
	Herbert S.W.	X		
	Howe F.			X
	Hoy W.			X
	Jones W.C.P.	X		
	Kennedy E.M.			X
	Kennedy M.	X		

CAPE MOUNTED RIFLEMEN Contd.

Rank	Name	Ba	Tr	Be
Cpl.	Lowe N.A.	X		
	Lowrey G.H.			X
	Mason H.			X
	Miller W.W.	X		
	Miskin W.E.	X		
	Monk G.			X
	Morrell H.			X
	Nightingale G.E.	X		
	O'Connor E.			X
	Orton C.	X		
	Parker F.	X		
	Parkes F.R.	X		
	Robertson J.	X		
	Robertson W.W.	X		
	Seaton W.G.	X		
	Smith R.	X		
	Snow F.	X		
	Stokes H.S.	X	X	
	Walters J.			X
	Wells J.	X		
	Wright J.	X		
Pte./Tpr.	Allen A.	X		
	Allison W.H.	X		
	Allman E.C.	X		
	Allman J.A.J.	X		
	Alred J.A.	X		
	Attewell T.	X		
	Avery J.	X		
	Baker T.S.	X		
	Barber J.	X		
	Bartnick C.	X		
	Baum F.			X
	Baxter W.	X		
	Beard E.F.			X
	Beaumont H.G.			X
	Beckerson W.	X		
	Beckles E.			X
	Bertenshaw B.	X		
	Bevan J.J.	X		
	Bicker-Caarten A.G.	X		
	Bicker-Caarten A.J.	X		
	Bird J.N.			X
	Bishop J.	X		
	Black W.	X		
	Borlace F.	X		
	Bowins G.	X		
	Bowles W.	X		X
	Bracken H.	X		
	Brayshaw H.R.	X		
	Bridges G.	X		

CAPE MOUNTED RIFLEMEN Contd.

		Ba	Tr	Be
Pte./ Tpr.	Brindle T.	X		
	Brod J.C.E.			X
	Broughton B.	X		
	Bruce C.W.	X		X
	Bruton G.W.	X		
	Bryce W.			X
	Büchner A.			X
	Bull J.	X		
	Burge G.A.			X
	Burns-Gibson W.G.			X
	Byrne W.A.	X	X	
	Cahill J.	X		
	Campbell A.E.			X
	Campbell D.	X	X	
	Campbell E.O.S.	X		
	Carnell F.G.	X		
	Carson H.W.	X		
	Carwithen S.			X
	Cassidy J.	X		
	Castles T.	X		X
	Channons J.	X		
	Chawner H.W.	X		
	Clegg T.W.	X		
	Clement C.	X		
	Cocker J.R.	X		
	Codrington G.			X
	Colebrook C.F.	X		
	Corfield T.W.	X		
	Coventry J.V.	X		
	Coventry W.	X		
	Crighton T.	X		
	Cross T.	X		
	Crowe H.	X		
	Cull J.	X		
	Cullinan J.J.	X		X
	Cumming R.N.	X		
	Currie R.E.			X
	Daniel S.R.	?	?	?
	Davis G.W.	X		
	Dawson W.Y.			X
	De Kock J.A.			X
	Dentry C.	X		
	Derges G.	X		
	Devereaux T.	X		
	Deverell E.J.	X		
	Dillon W.C.			X
	Dixon H.J.	X		
	Dobrowsky A.F.G.	X		
	Dodd A.			X
	Dodds A.	X		
	Dogherty J.	X		
	Downham J.	X		

CAPE MOUNTED RIFLEMEN Contd.

		Ba	Tr	Be
Pte./ Tpr.	Drayton T.	X	X	
	Drew A.			X
	Driver W.A.	X		
	Dunk W.	X		
	Dunn M.	X		
	Dyer R.H.			X
	Dyson G.H.	X		
	Eastwood J.	X		
	Eaton L.W.			X
	Ellerbeck D.	X		
	Elliot K.	X		
	Ellis C.W.	X		
	England W.E.O.	X		
	Esprey W.D.	X		X
	Evezard E.H.	X	X	
	Eyre A.	X		
	Eyre R.	X		X
	Finnis E.J.	X		
	Fisher H.M.	X		
	Fitzpatrick W.	X		
	Fletcher H.	X		
	Flint G.	X		
	Forder J.	X		
	Fowler A.E.	X		X
	Gardner F.C.	X	X	
	Garthorne R.R.			X
	Gettliffe S.			X
	Gill R.G.			X
	Gleeson T.P.	X		
	Goldwyn P.J.			X
	Goslin M.			X
	Gould N.	X		X
	Grant R.C.	X		
	Grant S.L.	X	X	
	Grapentin W.	X		
	Green G.			X
	Green T.J.	X		
	Greisbach F.T.R.		X	
	Grew T.	X		
	Hall S.C.	X		
	Hallovan A.			X
	Halsall A.		X	
	Hardy H.	X	X	
	Hargrove W.T.A.			X
	Harris A.A.	X		
	Harris J.S.			X
	Harrison A.	X		
	Harrison L.G.			X
	Harvey F.C.	X		
	Hawker C.A.			X
	Hayward W.	X		
	Headon C.F.	X		

17

CAPE MOUNTED RIFLEMEN Contd.

		Clasps		
		Ba	Tr	Be
Pte./ Tpr.	Heale E.M.			X
	Henderson A.E.K.			X
	Henning E.	X		
	Hersey W.	X		
	Heskins J.	X		
	Hill W.	X		
	Hingeston Randolph B.J.R.			X
	Hiscox J.R.	X		
	Hobson J.	X		
	Hodgson F.A.	X		
	Holmes R.	X		
	Homan W.	X		
	Hooley C.H.	X		
	Hooper E.R.			X
	Howell H.G.			X
	Hughes W.T.	X		
	Humphreys C.			X
	Hunter J.W.	X		
	Hunt Grubbe W.J.			X
	Hutt J.	X		
	Iggulden F.	X		
	Innes R.A.	X		X
	Jacobs S.J.			X
	Janion J.R.			X
	Jeffs C.H.	X		
	Jellicorse E.H.	X	X	
	Jenkins C.	X		
	Jolly J.B.	X		X
	Jones R.E.W.B.	X		
	Jones R.H.	X		
	Kearslake S.	X		
	Keating R.	X		
	Keeys W.	X		
	Kemp A.	X		
	Kernaghan J.	X		
	Kerridge G.F.	X		
	Kilcullen P.J.	X		
	King W.F.	X		
	King W.S.	X		
	Kloke C.	X		
	Koch C.J.	X		
	Krebs G.	X		
	Lambley J.T.			X
	Lamotte C.			X
	Landesman J.	X		
	Lane J.B.			X
	Last J.R.	X		
	Lee M.B.	X		
	Lee W.V.			X
	Lehmbeck W.H.			X
	Lewis R.	X		

CAPE MOUNTED RIFLEMEN Contd.

		Clasps		
		Ba	Tr	Be
Pte./ Tpr.	Lieberum J.W.	X		
	Loder E.I.			X
	Lonergan J.	X		
	Lupton-Smith W.	X		
	Lynch M.			X
	Marsden W.	X		
	Marsden W.H.	X		X
	Martin J.			X
	Martin S.E.			X
	Mason J.	X		
	Maythorne H.	X		
	Mc Carthy T.	X		
	Mc Kay M.C.	X		
	Meadows W.M.			X
	Mildred C.			X
	Miles W.S.	X		
	Mills E.S.	X		
	Moffett W.A.	X		
	Monk W.A.	X		
	Moore J.F.			X
	Moorman G.	X		X
	Morse T.			X
	Moyse T.O.	X	X	
	Murphy J.	X		
	Naude T.J.			X
	Naylor G.	X		
	Nelson W.F.	X	X	
	Newburgh A.R.C.	X		
	North H.	X		
	North W.J.R.	X		
	Norton H.H.	?	?	?
	Ollett J.T.	X		
	O'Sullivan T.			X
	Oswald R.C.			X
	Oxley A.	X		
	Palmer G.	X		
	Pearson E.F.			X
	Pearson T.	X		X
	Pease R.	X		
	Pedgrift H.A.A.	X		
	Phelan J.			X
	Poetsch C.	X		
	Powles K.F.			X
	Pratt J.A.	X		
	Prendergast H.Y.D.			X
	Pritchard A.	X		
	Pruen W.B.	X		
	Purcell J.F.	X		
	Quick J.	X		
	Reardon J.D.	X		
	Richards W.C.	X		

CAPE MOUNTED RIFLEMEN Contd.

Rank	Name	Ba	Tr	Be
Pte./Tpr.	Roberts A.R.	X		
	Roberts C.	X		
	Roberts J.	X		
	Robinson E.	X		
	Rosewall T.	X		
	Rowlands L.	X		
	Ryan J.	X		
	Salmond T.R.			X
	Sandwith H.F.M.	X		
	Savage J.H.			X
	Scott A.T.	X		
	Seager B.P.			X
	Setchell F.	X		
	Shannon P.			X
	Shaw E.	X		
	Shutler H.	X		
	Sikes J.H.			X
	Skelton C.	X		
	Skidmore W.	X		
	Smith C.	X		
	Smith G.	X		
	Smith J.	X		
	Smyth H.C.	X		
	Somerset H.E.	X		
	Sparrow A.B.	X	X	
	Springett F.J.	X		
	Steele A.	X		
	Steward A.	X	X	
	Stewart H.G.	X		
	Storey G.H.C.			X
	Taylor A.G.	X		
	Taylor J.			X
	Taylor W.J.	X		
	Telfer G.	X	X	
	Tetley F.J.			X
	Teverson H.R.	X		
	Thompson H.F.	X		
	Tideswell J.	X		
	Tincknell B.	X		
	Todd P.W.B.	X		
	Townshend J.G.	X		
	Tutchell C.			X
	Twiss C.W.	X		
	Varley H.C.	X		
	Vasey A.C.	X		
	Wakerley G.J.		X	
	Waldron F.	X		
	Walsh J.	X		
	Walsh R.E.			X
	Weatherilt H.C.	X		
	Webb C.	X		
	Webster W.	X		
	Welchman H.	X		
	White A.F.			X

CAPE MOUNTED RIFLEMEN Contd.

Rank	Name	Ba	Tr	Be
Pte./Tpr.	White E.	X		
	White E.P.	X		
	White F.I.	X		
	White P.	X		
	Wicker J.	X		
	Wiggans W.P.	X		
	Williams C.		X	
	Williams H.	X		
	Williams P.A.	No	Clasps	
	Wills W.H.	X		
	Witham T.H.			X
	Wood J.	X		
	Woods F.	X	X	
	Worby W.	X		
	Young	X		

CAPE MOUNTED YEOMANRY

Also listed as: C.M. Yeo
Cape Yeo 1st C.M. Yeo
2nd C.M. Yeo 3rd Cape
Yeo 3rd Yeomanry

Rank	Name	Ba	Tr	Be
Colonel.	Brabant E.Y.	X		
	Southey R.G.	X		
Surgeon.	Lamb R.G.	X		
Capt.	Catton W.T.	X	X	
	Chiappini A.L.	X	X	X
	Dalgety E.H.	X		X
	Durie W.	X	X	
	Feather T.R.	X		
	Ellis O.H.	X		
	Hudson C.R.	X		
	Kannemeyer H.M.	X		
	Kyd T.	X		
	Leach C.W.	X		
	Mullins P.	X		
	Smith H.M.	X		
	Sprigg H.	X		
	Stone H.M.	X		
	Stretton J.K.	X		
	Van Ryneveld W.C.	X	X	
	Vincent L.L.	X		
	White H.	X		
Lt.	Badger E.	X		
	Brady A.R.	X		
	Brady J.	X		
	Callender C.E.	X		
	Cock T.T.	X		
	Dawson W.R.	X		
	Fincham F.P.	X		

CAPE MOUNTED YEOMANRY Contd.

Rank	Name	Ba	Tr	Be
Lt.	Fink C.	X		
	Fletcher A.A.	X		
	Frost W.C.	X		
	Heugh P.R.	X		
	Kirkpatrick W.G.	X	X	
	Kruuse P.M.	X		
	Marshall G.	X		X
	Maynier H.F.W.	X		
	Pratt W.J.	X		X
	Schultz C.A.W.	X	X	
	Stirton G.	X		
	White W.N.	X		
Sgt./Maj.	Batteson G.W.	X		
	Berry P.	X		
	Clendinning J.H.		X	
	Damant F.W.	X		
	Doyle W.K.	X		X
	Evens A.C.	X		
	Flanagan P.J.	X		
	Gill E.J.	X		
	Goddard W.	X		
	Hood R.	X		
	Keeney A.	X		
	Parkin R.C.	X		
	Ridgway C.W.	X		
	Smith G.E.	X		
	Stretton G.A.	X		
	Warren G.J.	X		
	Webster W.E.	X		
	Weeks W.	X		
	Wright E.	X		
	Zietsman W.C.	X		
Qms.	Lux H.	X		
Sgt.	Albrecht L.W.	X		X
	Ballard W.F.	X		
	Barrable D.S.	X		
	Baxter C.	X		
Sgt. 1st Class	Booty W.F.S.	X		
Sgt.	Boss A.A.	X		
	Campbell F.	X		
	Clarke C.E.	X		
	Cogan R.J.	X	X	
	Dold W.J.	X		
	Dunn H.	X		
	Freemantle J.H.	X		
	Frost A.H.	X		
	Harding P.J.	X		

CAPE MOUNTED YEOMANRY Contd.

Rank	Name	Ba	Tr	Be
Tpt./Maj.	Hill C.	X		
Sgt.	Hill D.R.	X		
	Leach J.C.	X		
	Mc Donald W.	X		
	Meier W.F.	X		
	Meyer P.G.	X		
	Shaw J.W.	X	X	
	Van Wyke H.J.	X		
Saddler Sgt.	Weatherhead G.J.	X		
Sgt.	Webb T.K.	X		
Cpl.	Altenkirch J.	X		
	Binter E.G.	X		
	Blumrick F.C.	X		
	Botha F.J.	X		
	Brown D.	X		
	Burger W.	X		
	Clark W.M.	X	X	
	Cockin F.H.	X		
	Cogan A.W.	X		
	Cooper J.P.	X		
	Copeling R.W.	X		
	du Toit J.C.P.	X		
	Ebner H.A.	X		
	Erasmus P.A.	X		
	Goldswain C.E.	X		
	Herbert R.S.	X		
	Ingram W.	X		
	Jakins S.J.	X		
	Johnson J.G.G.	X		
	Landrey A.E.P.	X		
	Miles A.J.	X		
	O'Brien G.S.	X	X	
	Pearson T.	X		
	Rademeyer N.P.	X		
	Rahn J.	X		
	Schrieber G.	X		
	Smithdorf G.	X		
	Sutherland D.J.	X	X	
	Van Coller C.A.	X		
	Vorster J.P.	X		
	Walsh J.	X		
	Webster H.G.	X		
	Wells H.H.	X		
	Wollenschlaeger W.	X		
Bugler	Bennett J.	X		
	Bold R.W.	X		
	Boyle J.	X		
	Holmes J.A.	X		

CAPE MOUNTED YEOMANRY Contd.

		Clasps		
		Ba	Tr	Be
Pte./	Andrews J.J.	X		
Tpr.	Bauer F.	X		
	Bauer J.	X		
	Beer R.	X		
	Bishop W.	X		
	Bloomer E.	X		
	Blumrick C.W.	X		
	Bold J.	X		
	Botha I.P.	X		
	Brandon A.J.	X		
	Brent C.H.	X		
	Brent H.B.	X		
	Brink J.G.	X		
	Brooks E.L.	X		
	Brown H.A.	X		
	Bruce C.V.	X		X
	Bruce G.H.	X		
	Bubb J.	X		
	Buist C.M.	X		
	Buss A.	X		
	Butters A.	X		
	Campbell C.J.	X		
	Capper T.	X		
	Carney A.E.	X		
	Carruthers J.	X		
	Causebrook J.	X		
	Crole A.C.	X		
	Culley W.H.	X		
	Cunningham J.A.	X		
	Cunningham W.	X		
	Damant G.C.	X		
	Danoher J.	X		
	Davies A.	X		
	Deconing C.J.	X		
	Dent T.	X		
	Dobrousky A.	X		
	Duffield G.H.	X		
	Edwards W.J.	X		
	Eliott J.	X	X	
	Ellis P.J.M.	X	X	
	Feitz L.	X		
	Felton W.J.	X		
	Ferreira D.T.	X		
	Ferreira I.M.	X		
	Ferreira J.F.	X		
	Fisher A.J.	X		
	Fitchet D.A.	X		
	Fitzgibbons J.	X		
	Frier A.	X		
	Fuller W.H.	X		
	Gill G.	X		

CAPE MOUNTED YEOMANRY Contd.

		Clasps		
		Ba	Tr	Be
Pte./	Gill W.J.	X		
Tpr.	Goldswain A.H.	X		X
	Goldswain E.E.	X		
	Grapentin H.	X		
	Grobler N.J.	X		
	Grobler T.	X		
	Harding J.	X		
	Harris T.R.	X		
	Hawkins J.H.	X		
	Hawkins W.	X		
	Heathcote H.F.	X		
	Heydenrych W.J.	X		
	Heydruyck W.G.	X	X	
	Hill H.	X		
	Hohman J.	X		
	Holder H.A.		X	
	Holmes J.	X		
	Hopt G.	X		
	Hoskin J.W.	X		X
	Howe G.F.	X		
	Howe H.	X		
	Hurley P.	X		
	James G.H.	X		
	Jenkinson E.D.	X		
	Jenkinson J.J.	X		
	Jennings R.B.	X		
	Kayser S.T.C.	X		X
	Keogh S.S.	X		
	Kessler P.	X		
	Killick W.H.W.	X		
	Kleinhaus H.T.	X		
	Knowles T.	X		
	Koch J.D.	X		
	Kreedeman G.	X		
	Kritzinger L.R.	X		
	Kumm F.F.	X		
	Lane J.	X		
	Lavin E.H.	X		
	Leiberum H.	X		
	Luck C.F.	X		
	Marz H.F.	X		
	Massey J.	X		
	Maytham A.	X		
	Maytham M.J.	X		
	Mc Callum A.	X		
	Mc Donald D.C.	X		
	Mc Guire E.	X	X	X
	Mc Lean H.C.	X		
	Millborrow R.H.	X		
	Mitchley A.S.	X		
	Monteith R.	X		

CAPE MOUNTED YEOMANRY Contd.

		Ba	Tr	Be
Pte./ Tpr.	Moran J.E.	X		
	Morgan J.D.	X		
	Muldoon J.	X		
	Munro G.R.	X		
	Myburgh J.J.	X		
	Nelson A.	X	X	
	Nesemann H.	X		
	Oliver H.T.B.	X	X	
	Pagel C.F.	X		
	Pedlar C.W.	X		
	Petser H.	X		
	Petzer S.	X		
	Pocart W.	X		
	Pocock W.	X	X	
	Potgieter M.E.	X		
	Potgieter P.H.	X		
	Promnitz T.	X		
	Purdon E.A.	X	X	
	Querl E.	X	X	
	Quinn F.T.	X	X	
	Rawstorne J.	X		
	Roberts F.M.W.	X		
	Roebert C.A.	X		
	Roome E.A.	X		
	Rowley G.	X		
	Ryan J.J.	X		
	Salzwedel H.E.	X		
	Sanders G.	X		X
	Sawyer J.C.	X		
	Schmidt J.	X		
	Schrieber A.	X		
	Schrieber H.	X		
	Schrieber P.J.	X		
	Schröder H.	X		
	Schroeder W.	X		
	Smith C.	X		
	Smith H.	X		
	Smith S.	X		
	Snyman M.J.	X		
	Solomon J.W.	X	X	
	Stanton W.E.	X		
	Stowe J.	X		
	Strutt R.F.A.	X		X
	Taylor F.	X	X	
	Unteedt F.W.	X		
	Van Broemlsen O.	X	X	
	van der Merwe W.	X		
	van der Watt R.	X		
	van der Westhuize N.J.	X		
	van Niekerk C.P.J.	X		
	van Niekerk J.S.J.	X		

CAPE MOUNTED YEOMANRY Contd.

		Ba	Tr	Be
Pte./ Tpr.	van Onselen G.C.	X		
	van Oselen S.H.	X		
	van Rooyen P.L.	X		
	van Staaden C.J.	X	X	
	van Tonder A.J.	X		
	van Winkel N.D.	X		
	van Wyke D.J.	X	X	
	Vice C.J.	X		
	Vickers J.J.	X		
	Warner F.W.	X		
	Warren R.J.G.	X	X	
	Warren T.H.	X		
	Webb I.	X		
	Webster E.E.	X		
	Wesson T.	X		
	West W.	X		
	Willard C.	X		
	Williams T.	X		
	Willmer F.	X		
	Wilmouth J.P.	X		
	Wilson C.F.	X		
	Winkelmann A.	X		
	Winkelmann E.	X		
	Wise T.	X		
	Wollenschlager	X		
	Wood J.	X		
	Wright A.W.	X		
	Wynne W.J.	X		
	Yorke H.	X		
	Zeller J.T.	X		

Office of the Commissioner of Police
District No. 1
King Williams Town
9th July 1900

The Secretary to the Law Department
CAPE TOWN.

Sir,

NOMINAL ROLL OF CAPE POLICE DIST. No. 1
AND SPECIAL EUROPEAN AND NATIVE POLICE
ATTACHED THERETO ENGAGED IN THE
BECHUANALAND CAMPAIGN 1896/97

Pursuant to the instructions contained in your letter N.C. 3/331 of the 2nd instant, I have the honour to submit herewith, roll as above, the details figuring in which are shown in the different ranks in which they served in the campaign in question.

I have placed the names of Lieut. E.C. Powell and No. 35 Private Ackerman in the roll, though seeing that both were compelled through illness, to return from the Homestead Camp at Kimberley. I am not in a position to say if they are entitled to the medal.

Lt. Albrecht was detached for special duty under the late Colonel Lanning during the rebellion.

I have the honour to be
Sir
Your obedient-servant

Daniell

Commissioner Commanding C.P.

AUTHOR'S NOTE:

With this letter, lists, containing 1048 names of all ranks were submitted.

CAPE POLICE DISTRICT No. 1.

		Clasps		
		Ba	Tr	Be
Capt.	Foy L.A.		X	X
	Neylan J.N.			X
	Tainton A.P.	X		X
	Wilson A.C.			X
Lt.	Ayliff W.E.	X		X
	Berrange C.A.L.	X		X
	Bovey W.R.			X
	Bridge W.S.			X
	Cowie C.R.			X
	Cowie J.H.			X
	Delaney T.			X
	Gillwald F.W.H.	X	X	X
	Halse G.B.			X
	Harvey A.St. J.			X
	Harvey F.W.			X
	Hayes H.	X		X
	Powell C.M.			X
	Powell E.G.			X
	Reid G.S.B.			X
	Sampson S.J.			X
	Tainton R.A.K.			X
	Vincent F.A.			X
RSM.	Cumming J.R.			X

Sgt.

		Ba	Tr	Be
228	Allison P.J.			X
17	Butler F.			X
434	Cahill M.			X
340	Charters W.H.			X
9	Clacke E.A.S.			X
506	Denyssen H.J.			X
1	Doyle F.T.			X
224	Durandt P.W.			X
335	Dye E.H.	X	X	X
3	Eastes J.W.			X
428	Fisher W.			X
7	Fuller W.H.			X
16	Halse T.H.			X
14	Kayser R.F.W.			X
587	Kramer A.E.			X
498	Moony J.W.O.E.			X
429	Muller I.J.		X	X
381	Nicholas J.			X
383	Saunderson T.	X		X
223	Schley A.P.J.			X
496	Trautmann A.			X
338	Van Staden P.J.			X
497	Walker M.			X
230	Whelan S.C.			X
28	Woon E.W.			X

CAPE POLICE DISTRICT No. 1 Contd.

Cpl.

		Ba	Tr	Be
499	Attwood A.J.			X
157	Bailey H.			X
504	Bentley K.M.			X
501	Bovey E.			X
550	Christie R.B.			X
337	Devine W.D.			X
11	Durrheim A.			X
27	Els L.D.			X
19	Field S.H.			X
548	Fitzpatrick E.W.			X
338	Goldswain C.			X
152	Hamilton G.H.			X
150	Harvey A. Mc D.			X
236	Hewlett F.W.			X
387	Johnson E.E.			X
34	Keitzmann F.			X
147	Kuhn F.G.			X
435	Mc Winnie A.			X
545	Morgan O.V.			X
589	Nightingale F.L.			X
591	Pantz R.F.J.			X
382	Pittaway A.			X
26	Porter D.H.	X		X
592	Treadway G.G.H.			X
342	Vice E.A.			X
593	Wade A.H.			X
153	Walsh T.J.			X
549	Young W.A.			X

L./Cpl.

		Ba	Tr	Be
565	Allcock N.G.			X
444	Allnutt A.			X
855	Ammann F.			X
528	Anderson F.			X
904	Baines C.C.			X
277	Barnett A.J.P.			X
287	Barnett H.D.M.			X
449	Bergh W.F.			X
455	Beukes J.J.			X
390	Burrows M.			X
292	Cayton G.			X
345	Demmer L.J.			X
275	D'Ewes J.A.			X
184	de Villiers C.P.			X
508	Doyle J.H.K.			X
289	Dryden W.J.			X
61	Esprey W.D.			X
512	Fleischer S.W.			X
696	Fraser H.B.			X
??	Fynn M.D.			X

CAPE POLICE DISTRICT
No. 1 Contd.

L/Cpl.

No.	Name	Ba	Tr	Be
514	George A.			X
165	Glenister E.			X
274	Green E.A.			X
346	Harvey H.			X
700	Herley P.W.			X
168	Hertz V.A.			X
62	Hoft J.F.W.			X
520	Hooper D.H.			X
43	James C.A.			X
254	Jenkinson W. Mc.D.			X
12	Jones R.J.			X
570	Kemp P.C.			X
594	Kincaid J.			X
166	Kobus A.C.E.			X
52	Kuhn C.H.			X
442	Lawrence G.			X
450	Leppan W.E.			X
395	Liedtke C.H.T.			X
169	Lockhardt G.			X
164	Maggs J.D.			X
399	Marsden A.E.			X
54	Mc Cabe C.J.H.			X
465	Mc Lellan J.			X
518	Miller W.J.			X
??	Mullen S.H.			X
243	Nell L.J.M.			X
640	Newton T.C.			X
349	Niland E.			X
41	Rudolph H.F.W.			X
67	Rushton M.M.			X
408	Smith A.S.			X
170	Smith T.P.			X
467	Sprang J.L.			X
553	Squier J.			X
353	Thomas J.D.			X
597	Westbrook T.P.			X
397	Whitaker P.J.			X
57	White G.H.			X
604	Williams I.J.			X

Pte.

No.	Name	Ba	Tr	Be
295	Ackerman J.			X
35	Ackerman J.J.			X
1103	Adkins H.			X
358	Alesbury G.			X
1194	Alford J.B.			X
600	Alford P.A.			X
??	Antwerp F.C.			X
185	Armstrong W.H.G.			X

CAPE POLICE DISTRICT
No. 1 Contd.

No.	Name	Ba	Tr	Be
759	Arnold C.H.			X
596	Arnold R.			X
714	Arnold T.T.			X
1069	Attwell W.B.			X
1266	Baker J.			X
443	Baker T.H.			X
74	Batchelor R.H.			X
357	Belter H.F.			X
1016	Benn W.B.			X
294	Benette J.H.			X
??	Berg C.G.			X
954	Bisset H.W.			X
1243	Bloomfield W.A.			X
253	Blumrick E.A.			X
60	Booth J.			X
1067	Botha F.J.			X
719	Bovey H.			X
1117	Bowles A.O.			X
1029	Boyes S.H.			X
942	Boyle P.			X
1101	Brandt W.			X
1171	Braun S.			X
835	Briest A.			X
777	Brown B.W.			X
775	Brown G.M.			X
795	Brumsden W.T.			X
271	Brussouw E.J.C.			X
660	Buckley J.			X
1114	Campbell A.D.			X
343	Campbell W.D.			X
779	Canny J.			X
1163	Carney J.W.			X
858	Carswell J.C.			X
1269	Cawood H.E.			X
931	Clack G.F.			X
941	Clack J.			X
1157	Clevel C.			X
1271	Colley J.			X
1220	Comer F.			X
441	Connor O.			X
712	Cooks S.			X
656	Cumming A.			X
1225	Cumming G.			X
987	Cunze W.S.C.			X
1084	Darling W.			X
??	Davis W.J.			X
473	Dawson E.E.			X
453	de Beer Z.			X
1013	Deere R.H.			X
1007	Deering A.C.			X
848	Delport B.			X
248	Diesel J.C.W.			X

CAPE POLICE DISTRICT
No. 1 Contd.

Pte.		Ba	Tr	Be
866	Dobie J.C.			X
845	Drake W.			X
902	Dye J.B.			X
1087	Dye W.T.			X
921	Edy N.H.			X
964	Ekron W.H.			X
409	Eksteen H.			X
1020	Els C.W.			X
850	Els F.C.			X
352	Els J.M.			X
1074	Els J.M.			X
960	Els W.A.			X
1201	Emslie W.H.			X
741	Endres G.W.			X
1207	Evens H.C.W.			X
649	Ewers E.			X
650	Farrell J.P.			X
1288	Fennell C.O.			X
812	Fentham E.			X
729	Ferreira E.F.C.			X
766	Fielding R.C.			X
1213	Flynn J.P.			X
1195	Forbes T.E.B.			X
1229	Francis J.T.			X
??	Frauenstein F.			X
1092	Frauenstein R.			X
881	Freislich H.W.			X
1014	Geddes A.			X
997	George W.R.			X
398	Gill F.			X
979	Godfrey V.J.			X
469	Gradwell G.W.			X
1138	Graham F.L.			X
1162	Graham J.O.			X
651	Green J.H.			X
1044	Greyling J.			X
1234	Gunston T.			X
??	Hack R.H.			X
962	Hall A.P.			X
744	Halpin J.			X
963	Halse H.			X
392	Hambley A.			X
642	Hannibal H.			X
1215	Harris R.A.			X
694	Hart A.E.			X
??	Hartwig F.			X
873	Hatton R.H.			X
928	Hayward A.M.C.			X
773	Hearns W.R.			X
1059	Heidtman T.			X

CAPE POLICE DISTRICT
No. 1 Contd.

Pte.		Ba	Tr	Be
1107	Hendry F.A.			X
1156	Hennessy J.E.			X
1008	Hodge H.			X
1097	Holliday T.C.			X
1105	Hoskins C.H.			X
870	Howes A.M.			X
??	Hutchons E.S.			X
1240	Jeffersen C.			X
780	Jenner F.			X
787	Jenner L.W.			X
1049	Jennings A.			X
1253	Johnson C.			X
55	Jones J.			X
1036	Jones W.J.			X
563	Jorissen W.E.J.			X
610	Keen W.C.T.			X
856	Keightley P.G.			X
1230	Kemmendy E.			X
1045	Kenny J.			X
290	Kirton H.			X
65	Kleingeld J.M.			X
1119	Kobus C.W.			X
1278	Kokot M.F.			X
697	Kruger C.G.			X
1018	Kuhn G.			X
1151	Kukard C.F.W.			X
1273	Kukard F.F.G.			X
232	Kutchner J.W.			X
1236	Lamb H.O.			X
726	Lavin G.M.			X
32	Lesch E.			X
718	Lesch W.R.			X
1196	Levey S.A.			X
1043	Lewis G.H.			X
1035	Liefeldt N.W.			X
666	Littleford F.W.H.			X
808	Lloyd J.			X
635	Lloyd P.O.			X
854	Loder J.O.			X
464	Lund C.F.			X
1265	Mahood W.H.			X
1123	Mandy E.			X
677	Marais G.H.			X
810	Marais J.G.			X
757	Mardon J.C.			X
878	Marley J.H.			X
861	Mc Allister B.J.			X
1072	Meyer G.			X

CAPE POLICE DISTRICT No. 1 contd.

Pte.

No.	Name	Ba	Tr	Be
760	Mitten J.C.			X
965	Moffett G.H.			X
1268	Möller J.			X
1150	Moolman B.			X
1135	Mostert G.			X
1075	Mullen	X		
864	Muller S.H.			X
??	Mundy E.			X
733	Murray E.P.			X
410	Mynhardt J.			X
1190	Mynhardt S.J.D.			X
267	Naude J.A.			X
889	Nel J.J.D.			X
955	Nell S.F.			X
706	Nicholas F.			X
263	Niekerk C.J.H.			X
273	Niekerk J.H.			X
969	Oosthuizen H.P.			X
996	Packet W.			X
826	Parker T.E.			X
647	Paulick J.			X
1152	Peachey C.			X
402	Peacock W.			X
990	Pote P.			X
515	Prinsloo J.T.			X
917	Pugh C.F.			X
1286	Putzier W.A.			X
1259	Rafferty A.J.			X
466	Rathbone G.H.			X
517	Rautenbach P.G. (Shown on the Roll as Bautimbach P.G.)			X
737	Reed T.E.			X
525	Rensburgh M.H.			X
1003	Richards C.P.			X
703	Richardson H.D.			X
998	Riggs R.			X
1031	Ritchie A.			X
728	Roberts A.E.			X
816	Roberts H.F.			X
1028	Robinson J.W.			X
983	Roulstone T.			X
1280	Rouse E.			X
853	Rouw H.G.			X
1248	Rowland C.W.			X
988	Rudolph C.			X
762	Russon W.F.			X
445	Sampson S.A.			X
75	Sanders A.G.			X

CAPE POLICE DISTRICT No. 1 Contd.

Pte.

No.	Name	Ba	Tr	Be
1108	Sanson A.W.			X
180	Schroeder C.			X
672	Schroeder E.A.C.			X
906	Seeber C.R.			X
832	Seig J.			X
1180	Simpson H.N.			X
1004	Smith L.A.			X
1140	Smith P.W.			X
717	Smith S.C.			X
598	Somerset W.G.			X
1122	Stack T.			X
659	Stahl C.J.L.			X
1121	Staples A.W.			X
241	Steyn P.G.			X
1096	Stock H.W.			X
1010	Stockdale L.D.			X
1161	Stolz J.J.			X
1191	Strauch L.			X
??	Street J.W.			X
1270	Strohkirch G.			X
524	Strydom J.F.			X
830	Stubbs E.T.			X
451	Sutton A.J.			X
568	Swart M.D.O.			X
874	Sweetman E.J.			X
1023	Swemmer H.A.			X
1218	Tacey A.			X
1088	Terblans N.P.			X
909	Treadway E.C.			X
1176	Treadway H.J.			X
1149	Trollip L.C.			X
1173	van der Westhuizen C.			X
1065	van Onselen G.R.P.			X
1060	van Wyk H.C.			X
250	Wagener J.P.J.			X
702	Wallace A.D.			X
1241	Waterford C.S.			X
1125	Waters S.R.			X
438	Webber H.C.			X
391	Wheeler H.W.H.			X
389	White A.N.			X
716	Whittle A.E.			X
505	Young W.J.			X

Special Police.

	Name	Ba	Tr	Be
	de Villiers J.S.H.			X
	Farrell J.H.			X
	Fitzgerald E.D.			X
	Gallon E.L.			X

CAPE POLICE DISTRICT No. 1 Contd.

Special Police.

Name	Ba	Tr	Be
Hansen H.			X
Keen T.H.C.			X
Langdon J.			X
Longley W.			X
Miller M.A.			X
Poole H.T.			X
Reeland C.J.			X
Rutland C.J.			X
Scott J.A.			X
Smith A.A.	?	?	?

Native Detective.

Name	Ba	Tr	Be
Abram			X
August			X
Banjiwe			X
Bokwa			X
Booi			X
Breakfast			X
Breakfast M.			X
Dabadaba			X
Diamond			X
Dumezweni			X
Elijah			X
Frenchmen			X
Gonyama			X
Gxekwa			X
Impiyonke			X
January			X
Jonas M.			X
Kafir			X
Kali			X
Kleinbooi			X
Kleinbooi Nani			X
Kulu August			X
Letuka			X
Lynx			X
Naclean B.			X
Majamana			X
Makefa			X
Makisi			X
Malamba			X
Mata			X
Mputuma			X
Mhlanyana			X
Mkomo John			X
Neku Joel			X
Ngateni J.			X
Ntisi Charley			X

CAPE POLICE DISTRICT No. 1 Contd.

Native Detective.

Name	Ba	Tr	Be
Patrol			X
Shadrack			X
Silasi			X
Skenjani James			X
Solomon Philip			X
Tandimali			X
Tom Jim			X
Tomba J.			X
Walter			X
Witbooi			X
Xelegwana			X
Xonti William			X
Zeli Tom			X

Native Sgt.

No.	Name	Ba	Tr	Be
77	Makebe Joseph			X

Native Pte.

No.	Name	Ba	Tr	Be
1237	Aleki			X
324	Andrew			X
1188	April			X
1120	August			X
105	Baba William			X
??	Backai			X
315	Barnett			X
1227	Barnett Fred			X
80	Bartman George			X
316	Belmore Jim			X
202	Ben Mgadi			X
134	Blom			X
131	Booi			X
194	Booi			X
301	Booi Tom			X
98	Boots			X
325	Campbell			X
109	Captain			X
81	Chaka			X
307	Dante Sam			X
96	Diniso			X
818	Dolo Samuel			X
1165	Dumezweni			X
318	Elijah David			X
989	Fatela John			X
1011	Femele			X
1245	Feni Jacob			X
888	Frank			X
875	Gaika Christian			X
893	Gaika Henry			X
192	Gaveni			X

CAPE POLICE DISTRICT No. 1 Contd.

Native Pte.

No.	Name	Ba	Tr	Be
1143	George			X
926	Gege			X
1186	Gert Skewa			X
487	Ginda Tetani			X
493	Gunguluza			X
883	Gwabi James			X
1242	Harris John			X
191	Jafta			X
1146	Jantje			X
1111	Jantjie			X
1040	Jassap James			X
79	Jeke			X
1247	Jonas			X
296	Kleinbooi			X
1287	Kleinbooi			X
??	Kondhlo J.			X
419	Kovi			X
119	Kulu			X
422	Kulu			X
138	Lucas John			X
1021	Mageli			X
103	Mangali			X
616	Mati Jan			X
993	Matyila John			X
365	Max			X
475	Mbangi George			X
78	Meli Alfred			X
111	Mgenga Philip			X
122	Mgxunyeni			X
113	Mjo Paul			X
312	Mondelik			X
1211	Moses			X
195	Mpande			X
321	Msabenzie			X
82	Mtoba William			X
938	Mvalo			X
306	Ndita Tom			X
216	Nelani			X
857	Neli			X
112	Neuka James			X
1116	Ngculu			X
135	Ngie John			X
1064	Ngolobe Edward			X
529	Nguleni Mlambo			X
490	Ngwentle Alfred			X
102	Notoli			X
1128	Njol Jim			X
1224	Ntisiki			X

CAPE POLICE DISTRICT No. 1 Contd.

Native Pte.

No.	Name	Ba	Tr	Be
333	Nyati John			X
359	Nyokana John			X
1147	Olifant Jacob			X
93	Pacamite Jacob			X
1039	Patela			X
476	Peppetta Paul			X
84	Petros			X
376	Pony			X
??	Prince Zuma			X
781	Pulapi			X
827	Qobodoane			X
121	Qualgu John			X
117	Richard			X
212	Sam			X
371	Sam			X
327	Sdinana Josian			X
304	September H.			X
1178	Sigodo			X
95	Siko			X
1034	Simon			X
??	Skenjana P.			X
298	Skey			X
1129	Skulpat			X
1154	Skuyana Samuel			X
1000	Smile			X
104	Snaam W.			X
936	Sney			X
127	Sobekwa			X
1276	Sogiba George			X
482	Sogiba James			X
360	Solani			X
1130	Solomon			X
636	Songela			X
101	Songela			X
110	Stephen			X
952	Taylor			X
201	Thomas			X
811	Thomas			X
582	Thys			X
421	Tom			X
125	Tsomi John			X
1267	Tunzi David			X
885	Vapi			X
205	Veli			X
123	Vumani			X
126	Welcome			X
??	Williams T.			X
130	Windvogel			X

CAPE POLICE DISTRICT No. 1 Contd.

Native Pte.

		Clasps		
		Ba	Tr	Be
317	Windvogel			X
937	Zanazo			X
303	Zotchani			X

CAPE POLICE DISTRICT No. 2.

Rank	Name	Ba	Tr	Be
Inspector Capt.	Browne J.W.			X
	Snow A.B.			X
Lt.	Moorhead J.			X
Sub Insp.	Bates A.			X
	Elliott F.H.			X
	Murray A.D.			X
	Rush W.H.			X
Sgt./Maj.	Davidson T.M.			X
	Taylor W.			X
Sgt.	Beatty J.			X
	Brady C.G.			X
	Crosbie P.			X
	Graham R.W.			X
	Jolly J.B.			X
	Matthews E.J.			X
	McQuire G.			X
	Rutherford G.			X
	Shepherd G.			X
	Thorne W.R.B.			X
	Watermeyer F.E.			X
	White J. (No.16)			X
	White J.T. (No. 15)			X
	Williams C.F.			X
Cpl.	Monro D.			X
	Proctor W.			X
Pte.	Abrams S.			X
	Antwerp F.C.			X
	Armstrong J.E.			X
	Ashton W.			X
	Barck C.E.			X
	Barnes A.			X
	Barton D.			X

CAPE POLICE DISTRICT No. 2 Contd.

Rank	Name	Ba	Tr	Be
Pte.	Bawtree J.H.			X
	Beatty A.			X
	Beckwith P.			X
	Berry F.			X
	Bester F.P.			X
	Blair J.C.			X
	Brown A.J.			X
	Brown C.			X
	Brown P.			X
	Brown S.H.			X
	Bunce H.W.			X
	Burger G.P.			X
	Carlyle T.			X
	Chadwick R.			X
	Clark W.			X
	Clinkenbury P.			X
	Collins G.			X
	Corbett G.W.			X
	Court J.S.			X
	Coxwell E.W.			X
	Deane C.			X
	Erswell A.V.			X
	Etsebeth P.J.			X
	Fielding L.M.			X
	Finlay W.W.			X
	Frank F.F.			X
	Garrett G.H.			X
	Gash R.H.			X
	Gore W.			X
	Gorse W.R. (Should be George W.R.)			X
	Gow J.J.			X
	Grendon J.W.			X
	Hastie J.A.			X
	Hayes W.H.			X
	Hazelrigg A.			X
	Hillier W.H.			X
	Hillstroom F.			X
	Hipwell C.H.			X
	Hulbert W.			X
	Human J.L.			X
	Hynes W.			X
	Jack C.M.			X
	Jacobs W.D.			X
	Jones T.			X
	Judge E.			X
	Kuppers W.			X
	Leversage F.			X
	Lewis G. de B.			X
	Limerick J.St. C.			X

CAPE POLICE DISTRICT
No. 2 Contd.

		Clasps		
		Ba	Tr	Be
Pte.	Louw J.C.			X
	Maher J.L.			X
	Matthews J.			X
	Mc Gregor A.M.			X
	Merry H.C.			X
	Middleton C.E.			X
	Muller H.H.			X
	O'Brien J.			X
	O'Dell D.			X
	O'Dowd M.			X
	Okes H.T.			X
	Oosthuizen J.			X
	Peacock C.W.			X
	Pender W.			X
	Poynton H.J.			X
	Purchase H.J.			X
	Reardon J.J.			X
	Reynolds W.H.			X
	Richards A.W.			X
	Scally J.			X
	Sharrock W.			X
	Siebker G.A.			X
	Skinner R.L.			X
	Slatter T.			X
	Stallard E.			X
	Stearn A.			X
	Strauss P.M.D.			X
	Tarpey W.			X
	Thornley G.			X
	Toke C.W.			X
	Urbasch J.H.			X
	van der Merwe J.J.			X
	Venter J.P.			X
	Volkebron C.H.			X
	Von Witt W.S.J.			X
	Ward F.E.			X
	Ward W.			X
	Walker R.			X
	Wardle W.G.J.			X
	Warren H.T.			X
	Wilson C.D.			X
	Wimble C.E.			X
	Wilson G.			X

Special Police.

		Ba	Tr	Be
Cpl.	van Wyk A.			X
	Walker R.P.			X

CAPE POLICE DISTRICT
No. 2 Contd.

Special Police.

		Clasps		
		Ba	Tr	Be
Pte.	Agnew G.			X
	Atkins A.			X
	Beckett D.Mc P.			X
	Belstead E.J.			X
	Brauns H.W.			X
	Burnette F.			X
	Burt F.S.			X
	Calder V.			X
	Calder W.			X
	Campbell H.			X
	Cannell E.			X
	Carr A.			X
	Carter S.			X
	Coleman W.R.			X
	Dickenson W.			X
	Downing H.K.			X
	Dunk C.H.			X
	Durand D.J.			X
	Fisher A.H.			X
	Geane A.E.			X
	Giani A.E.			X
	Grace J.J.			X
	Hansen C.W.			X
	Hills W.H.			X
	Humphreys S.R.			X
	Hunt G.F.			X
	Jones E.R.			X
	Kearney J.			X
	Kruger J.A. (89)			X
	Kruger J.A. (90)			X
	Lee E.J.			X
	Lotter M.J.			X
	Marais W.J.			X
	Mc Coach J.A.			X
	Mc Kenzie R.S.			X
	Mc Lennan W.J.			X
	Meilandt H.			X
	Misdal A.H.			X
	Munro S.C.			X
	Orpen F.H.R.			X
	Pinnock R.			X
	Prichard W.M.			X
	Pringle C.S.			X
	Ryan F.K.			X
	Scott T.C.			X
	Short W.W.			X
	Skowronek C.S.F.			X

CAPE POLICE DISTRICT No. 2 Contd.

Special Police.

Rank	Name	Ba	Tr	Be
Pte.	Smidt W.			X
	Smith C.N.			X
	Smith W.H.			X
	Stanford E.R.			X
	Stephenson W.B.			X
	Stouffer W.H.			X
	Sullivan P.			X
	Swart H.J.			X
	Sweeny A.			X
	Tucker A.			X
	Ulrichsen O.A.			X
	v.d. Gryp F.			X
	Voules T.A.			X
	Warr H.			X
	Wedekind F.			X
	Welsh G.B.			X
	Wilson R.			X
	Winch F.B.			X

CAPE POLICE Listed in the Roll as Cape Police Unable to allocate to either D1 or D2

Rank	Name	Ba	Tr	Be
Capt.	Fuller J.W.			X
	Hennessy G.Pope			X
	Mc Gregor C.F.M.			X
	van Heerden J.N.			X
Lt.	O'Brien P.			X
	Powell E.S.			X
	Ricketts C.L.			X
Sub/Ins.	Musgrave W.A.R.			X
	Schutte R.F.			X
Drill Ins.	Blow T.			X
Sgt.	Ball J.J.			X
	Brown H.P.			X
	Crawford R.M.			X
	Fisher E.M.			X
	Fraser W.C.			X
	Geary W.J.			X
	Gerrard J.H.			X

CAPE POLICE Contd.

Rank	Name	Ba	Tr	Be
Sgt.	Gore-Clough C.M.			X
	Hemsworth J.M.W.			X
	Jenkins W.H.			X
	Kennedy W.			X
	Matthews E.J.			X
	Phillips A.M.			X
	van Eyssen D.			X
Cpl.	Lloyd W.F.			X
	Otto J.H.			X
	Quinn J.			X
L./Cpl.	Fynn M.D.			X
	Hartung O.			X
Pte.	Abrahms S.			X
	Adamson J.			X
	Barrat R.			X
	Blumrick E.H.			X
	Bowden S.V.			X
	Brown H.L.			X
	Burnette F.			X
	Carsons F.R.			X
	Chauncey A.			X
	Childs G.			X
	Coetzee G.J.			X
	Collins A.			X
	Davidson T.M.			X
	Donovan C.F.			X
	Eaton A.			X
	Fabling L.M.			X
	Fawcett A.			X
	Ferreira I.M.			X
	Ferreira J.F.			X
	Ferreira T.I.			X
	Fielding W.C.D.			X
	Fitzpatrick P.J.F.			X
	Francis H.C.			X
	Fukuzana D.			X
	Garde F.			X
	Gash T.			X
	Gerrard E.E.			X
	Gillott T.			X
	Glover A.			X
	Goulden W.B.R.			X
	Graham G.W.R.			X
	Graves A.S.			X
	Halling A.C.			X
	Hammond F.			X
	Harvard J.			X
	Hegter J.			X

	Clasps		
	Ba	Tr	Be
CAPE POLICE Listed in the Roll as Cape Police Unable to allocate to either D^1 or D^2			
Pte. Henderson W.J.			X
Henley F.J.			X
Hodgson U.B.			X
Holliday W.			X
Hope E.			X
Howell D.E.P.			X
Hulin F.C.R.			X
Jamieson C.			X
Jenkins H.H.			X
Jennings S.G.			X
Keen G.W.			X
Kellet T.Y.			X
Kongobe J.			X
Kleinbooi D.			X
Kutchner J.W.			X
Lamb H.O.			X
Leigh J.			X
Leslie J.D.			X
Loder A.C.			X
Mahon G.			X
Manifold W.			X
Mc Intosh E.Mc K.			X
Mc Kinley F.D.			X
Mc Lean T.			X
Meintjes H.A.H.			X
Mills J.W.P.			X
Mills W.T.			X
Moberley D.H.			X
Moller M.			X
Mordan F.			X
Muller E.A.			X
Muller C.B.			X
Mulligan J.H.			X
Nel A.H.			X
Oates C.H.			X
O'Connor J.			X
Oelschig J.H.			X
Opemshaw F.			X
Payne R.			X
Penning A.W.			X
Pike J.M.			X
Prior H.G.v/d M.			X
Quinn T.H.			X
Ralph J.			X
Schreiner J.			X
Smith C.M.			X
Smith J.G.			X
Spangenberg J.P.			X
Spencer C.E.W.			X
Steele N.G.			X

	Clasps		
	Ba	Tr	Be
CAPE POLICE Contd.			
Pte. Stephenson J.			X
Stewart W.N.			X
Street H.			X
Sybray J.			X
Van Lilyveldt H.			X
Venter P.J.			X
Ward J.			X
Waters S.R.			X
Webb H.H.			X
Weirich A.C.			X
Weirich H.J.			X
Whelehan T.C.R.			X
Whitaker M.			X
White J.G.			X
Wimble C.E.			X
Wittstock L.C.			X
CAPE TOWN HIGHLANDERS.			
Capt. Watermeyer J.H.H.			X
Lt. Berghuys H.C.			X
Smithers J.H.			X
Solomon F.H.			X
Sgt./Maj. Johnstone W.H.			X
Qms. Galloway D.			X
Csm. Gray T.A.			X
Sgt. Campbell P.			X
Crerar J.W.			X
Gamble R.			X
Mc Cartney G.			X
Ormes C.O.E.			X
Wilmott E.F.			X
Cpl. Colenso A.			X
Elder A.			X
Hay J.			X
Lister H.			X
Mac Donald A.			X
Parker E.			X
Town J.M.			X
Stephens H.			X
L/C Bugler.			
Adair W.			X

CAPE TOWN HIGHLANDERS. Contd.

		Clasps		
		Ba	Tr	Be
L/Cpl.	Farrall J.D.			X
	Jeffery G.			X
	Newlands J.			X
	Reid J.			X
	Stephen A.			X
L/Cpl.	Wilson A.			X
Drum.				
Pte.	Adamson G.E.			X
	Applin C.			X
	Atkinson A.			X
	Ballantine H.F.			X
	Barrow A.			X
	Beer F.E.			X
	Bingley J.			X
	Birbeck G.J.			X
	Birch J.			X
	Bismead H.			X
	Bland A.D.			X
	Brinton A.A.			X
	Brooks J.A.			X
	Burns S.			X
	Cardinal V.J.C.			X
	Chenal E.M.			X
	Clayton J.G.B.			X
	Clementson H.L.			X
	Cooke J.J.			X
	Crouch T.M.B.			X
	Dawson R.			X
	Denny E.B.			X
	Duffy B.			X
	Dunn J.			X
	Fraser J.A.			X
	Gath J.W.			X
	Graham B.H.			X
	Grieve R.			X
	Gunn W.B.W.			X
	Hadaway A.F.			X
	Hayes J.			X
	Hewitt N.B.			X
	Hine A.T.			X
	Holland G.			X
	Jones T.			X
	Jones W.W.			X
	Kent J. (listed as J.K.Milroy)			X
	Kriger J.H.R.			X
	Kuhlman J.H.			X
	Lorimer D.D.			X

CAPE TOWN HIGHLANDERS. Contd.

		Clasps		
		Ba	Tr	Be
Pte.	Lorimer W.F.			X
	Lucas E.W.			X
	Mac Donald A.			X
	Mac Donald J.			X
	Mac Leod J.C.			X
	Mc Calla H.J.			X
	Mc Donald A.			X
	Mc Kay E.D.			X
	Mc Phail N.			X
	Mc Vean J.			X
	Mason F.			X
	Murphy F.P.			X
	Nicholl A.			X
	O'Neill R.			X
	Parkes F.G.			X
	Pelton R.			X
	Price G.F.			X
	Ralston H.M.			X
	Ramsay F.W.			X
	Ramsden J.H.			X
	Reams J.H.			X
	Revell C.H.			X
	Ross W.G.			X
	Rouse S.			X
	Rowley G.W.			X
	Sillifant D.J.			X
	Smith F.			X
	Smith F.R.			X
	Soderberg K.V.			X
	Summers R.			X
	Symes T.			X
	Thompson H. (555)			X
	Thompson H. (230)			X
	Tier J.G.			X
	Timmins W.			X
	Tomlin G.			X
	Toms C.W.			X
	Waller W.H.			X
	Walsh T.			X
	Waters R.J.B.			X
	Wilkinson J.R.			X
	Wulff G.J.			X

CAPE TOWN RANGERS.

		Ba	Tr	Be
Capt.	Nelson J.P.	X	X	
Lt./Adj.				
	Barker F.H. St.J.	X	X	

CAPE TOWN RANGERS. Contd.

		Clasps		
		Ba	Tr	Be
Lt.	Godwin E.E.	X	X	
	Tennant J.D.	X	X	
S/Maj.	Holyoak A.F.	X	X	
Sgt.	Begg A.F.	X	X	
	Brown J.A.	X	X	
	Mahony M.		X	
Cpl.	Horsburgh J.	X	X	
Pte.	Adriaanzen J.	X	X	
	Alexander F.R.	X	X	
	Attwell R.J.	X	X	
	Bassingthwaighte A.W.	X	X	
	Bouillon J.P.	X	X	
	Benson L.B.	X	X	
	Bentzen C.	X	X	
	Clinton J.		X	
	Forssell F.	X	X	
	Gould M.	X	X	
	Grondahl H.	X	X	
	Henderson W.	X	X	
	Hutten W.A.	X	X	
	Kelly H.	X	X	
	Mathieson C.H.	X	X	
	Mc Leod G.	X	X	
	Mc Kinon H.W.	X	X	
	Miller W.H.	X	X	
	Mosely M.J.	X	X	
	Patterson F.H.		X	
	Pike S.	X	X	
	Raymond J.	X	X	
	Solomon R.	X	X	
	Turnbull J.	X	X	
Bugler	van der Schyff J.P.	X	X	
Pte.	Van Niekerk D.	X	X	
	Wagner H.E.F.	X	X	
	Ward B.	X	X	
	Whyte H.	X	X	
	Whyte R.	X	X	
	Willemite W.D.	X	X	X
	Wills A.C.	X	X	
	Wyeth G.W.	X		
	Zinn J.	X	X	

CAPE TOWN RIFLES.

		Clasps		
		Ba	Tr	Be
Capt.	Hosmer E.A.C.	X		
	Seagrave O.N.	X		
Lt.	Dremel S.	X		
	Honey J.W.	X		
Q/Master.				
	Hare G.L.	X		
Sgt./Maj.	Frost J.B.	X		
Col. Sgt.	Diamond J.	X		
Sgt.	Hoffman G.A.	X	X	
	Knowles G.B.	X		
	Mc Evoy W.	X		
Cpl.	Richmond J.J.	X		
Pte.	Allison H.	X		
	Bone C.	X		
	Bosman H.C.	X		
	Brenster G.H.	X		
	Capes C.J.	X		
	Clausen C.	X		
	de Loit J.	X		
	Freeman W.J.	X		
	Gaffney W.	X		
	Goldrick T.	X		
	Gresham T.	X		
	Hellet H.	X		
	Hendricks H.J.	X		
	Hunter R.S.	X		
	le Seur J.J.	X		
	Linde L.	X		
	Lord T.	X		
	Mc Crate R.	X		
Bugler.				
	Mc Mullin H.J.	X		
Pte.	Mohrein F.	X		
	Moller H.P.	X		
	Mondt E.	X		
	Muizenheimer A.	X		
	Muizenheimer M.	X		
	O'Brein T.	X		
	Petersen C.	X		
	Petersen I.	X		

CAPE TOWN RIFLES. Contd.

Rank	Name	Ba	Tr	Be
Pte.	Piettersen J.	X		
	Quinne R.	X	X	X
	Riley J.	X		
	Roberts J.	X		
	Rumble C.	X		
	Schmidt P.F.	X		
	Schoonraad J.J.		X	
	Smith J.K.	X		
Bugler.	Smith T.	X		
Pte.	Stephens J.	X		
	Toole L.	X		
	Vine W.	X		
	Wilson P.	X		

CAPE TOWN VOLUNTEER ARTILLERY

Rank	Name	Ba	Tr	Be
Gnr.	Mackinnon D.		X	

CAPE TOWN VOLUNTEER ENGINEERS

Rank	Name	Ba	Tr	Be
Maj.	Serrurier C.G.	X	X	
	Tennant J.		X	
Lt.	Whitley G.H.		X	
Sgt./Maj.	Ryan J.P.		X	
Sgt.	Beehre W.T.		X	
	Bright H.F.		X	
	Hickey G.F.		X	
	Higgs G.E.		X	
Cpl.	Alexander J.		X	
	Batten H.W.		X	
	Emanudson J.A.		X	
	Higgs J.T.		X	
	Jansen J.I.		X	
	Keenan W.H.		X	
	Palmer H.		X	
	Surrurier A.J.Y.		X	
	Wilson W.		X	
	Woolward J.D.		X	
L/Cpl.	Carey T.J.		X	
	Patrick R.		X	
	Ross G.W.		X	
	Withiel S.		X	

CAPE TOWN VOLUNTEER ENGINEERS Contd.

Rank	Name	Ba	Tr	Be
Spr.	Andrews G.W.C.		X	
	Boltman F.W.		X	
	Bruce H.J.		X	
Pte.	Calmeyer F.		X	
	Calmeyer G.		X	
Spr.	Chaney		X	
	Cleenverck A.E.		X	
	de Vries P.		X	
	Diamond J.		X	
Pte.	Coldrey F.C.		X	
	Fotheringham A.A.		X	
Spr.	Gaum F.L.		X	
Bgle.	Heslop G.B.		X	
Spr.	Heydenryth M.		X	
	Leary F.G.		X	
	Mc Arthur R.	X	X	X
	Michael C.		X	
	Morgenrood H.		X	
	Roodt P.J.		X	
	Rutter C.		X	
	Taylor J.		X	
	Townshend A.W.		X	
	Vos M.		X	
	Wahl J.E.		X	
Pte.	Wedel H.A.		X	
Spr.	Williams M.J.		X	
Pte.	Wilter P.L.		X	
Spr.	Wilson T.J.	X	X	
Pte.	Woodhead R.A.		X	

CATHCART BURGHERS.

Rank	Name	Ba	Tr	Be
Capt.	Smith G.B.	X	X	
Sgt./Maj.	Mennigke C.F.F.	X	X	
Qms.	Bentley W.D.	X	X	
Sgt.	Barnes A.S.	X	X	
Cpl.	Hart J.R.	X		
Pte.	Fitzgibbon J.E.	X		

	Clasps		
	Ba	Tr	Be

CERES BURGHERS.

		Ba	Tr	Be
Cpl.	Woods W.S.		X	
Tpr.	Keet B.G.		X	
	Madden M.J.		X	
	Muir A.		X	
	Newbold J.		X	
	Theron P.L.		X	

CHALUMNA MOUNTED VOLS.
Also listed as
CHALUMNA VOL. CHALUMNA VOL. CAVALRY.

		Ba	Tr	Be
Capt.	Warren T.H.	X		
Lt.	Forrester R.W.	X		
Sgt.	Holl J.H.C.	X		
Tpr.	Rassmussen J.W.	X		
	Wright A.	X		

COLESBERG BURGHERS.
Also listed as
COLESBURG VOLS.

		Ba	Tr	Be
Capt.	Officer W.	X		
	Robertson A.	X		
Lt.	Von Maltetz L.J.F.	X		
Cpl.	Hopley W.M.	X		
	Kemper G.L.E.	X		
Pte.	Partridge S.W.	X		X
	Watts T.S.	X		
	Wells E.	X		
	Wells J.	X		

COLONIAL FORCES.

Commandant General.

		Ba	Tr	Be
	Griffith C.D.	X		

Paymaster General.

		Ba	Tr	Be
	Garcia A.H.	X		

Medical Officer.

		Ba	Tr	Be
	Barry H.	X		

Chief Staff Officer.

		Ba	Tr	Be
Maj.	Cochrane W.F.D.	X	X	

COLONIAL FORCES Contd.

Commandant General's Staff.

No Rank.

		Ba	Tr	Be
	Bickley J.	X		

COMMISSARIAT DEPT.
Also listed as COMM. & TRANSPORT.

		Ba	Tr	Be
Col.Com.	Nelson C.E.	X	X	

Commissariat Officer.

		Ba	Tr	Be
	Burrowes W.H.	X		

Deputy Comm.

		Ba	Tr	Be
	Hay A.B.	X	X	
	Millbourne J.C.	X		

Asst.Col.Comm.

		Ba	Tr	Be
	Evatt M.A.		X	
	Homer E.	X		
	Morgan N.A.	X		
	Thacker T.J.	X		

Asst.Comm.

		Ba	Tr	Be
	Cheetham F.G.	X	X	
	Pentland J.	X	X	
	Smith R.	X		X
	Welstead			X
Capt.	Poole			X
	Sissison J.	X	X	

Conductor.

		Ba	Tr	Be
	Wardle J.	X		
Sgt.	Ferns H.C.			X
	Ronaldson J.			X
Clerk.	Hastings C.F.			X
	Wright G.A.			X
Pte.	Wright J.H.	X	X	
Tpr.	Young W.K.			X

No Rank

		Ba	Tr	Be
	Cotes W.		X	
	Lacey B.M.	X		
	Orwin F.H.	X		
	Proctor J.J.	X		

COMMISSARIAT DEPT.
Also listed as COMM. & TRANSPORT Contd.

Storekeeper.

		Clasps		
		Ba	Tr	Be
	Bentall O.	X		X
	Bond A.M.		X	
	Jones E.		X	
	Lichfield P.E.	X		

CRADOCK BURGHERS
Also listed as:
CRADOCK INFANTRY
CRADOCK VOLUNTEERS
CRADOCK VOLUNTEER RIFLES

		Ba	Tr	Be
Capt.	Campbell A.v L.	X		
Lt.	Rattray W.G.	X		
Qms.	Hinds G.H.	X		
Sgt.	Henry E.B.	X		
	Joslin T.G.	X		
	Rawstorne J.G.	X		
	Thackuray	X		
	Webber G.D.	X		
	Prior E.W.D.	X		
Cpl.	Mc Quilkin J.S.	X		
	Rowland E.H.	X		
Pte.	Aspinall G.L.	X		
	Baird J.	X		
	Burnard E.	X		
Bugler.	Holmes J.A.	X		
Pte.	Holmes M.G.	X		
	Holmes M.J.	X		
	Hulley T.B.	X		
	Park C.R.	X		
	Trollip H.	X		
	Wright A.J.	X		X

DENNISONS HORSE.

		Ba	Tr	Be
Capt.	Hannay W.A.			X
Tpr.	Bredenkamp J.F.			X

DENNISONS HORSE Contd.

		Ba	Tr	Be
Pte.	Britz J.J.J.			X
	Demo J.			X
	Engelbrecht W.J.			X
	Fick J.			X
	Sadler A.C.			X

BASUTU CONTG.

		Ba	Tr	Be
Scout.	Makjane M.	X		
	Moletsanie P.	X		
	Mulatorew W.	X		

DESPATCH RIDER.

		Ba	Tr	Be
Qms.	Howman J.			X
Cpl.	Harrison C.			X
Tpr.	Illingworth E.			X
	May C.			X
	Roberts H.C.			X
Pte.	Rodel G.			X

Civilian

		Ba	Tr	Be
	Wallace W.T.E.	X		

DIAMOND FIELDS ARTILLERY

		Ba	Tr	Be
Lt.	Claude A.J.			X
	Raydon C.J.			X
Sgt./Maj.	Broderick J.			X
Qms.	Marsh A.E.			X
Sgt.	Glennie J.A.			X
	Hird A.W.			X
	Kidd A.			X
	Morphy J.L.			X
	Osborne J.P. (apparently served with R/E)	X		
Cpl.	Kelly A.F.			X
	Nicholson P.			X
Driver.	Hill J.H.J.			X
	Holmes A.			X

DIAMOND FIELDS ARTILLERY Contd.

		Clasps	
	Ba	Tr	Be
Pte. Humphrys S.R.			X
Gunner.			
Anderson E.			X
Broderick W.J.			X
Deary J.N.			X
Ellison G.W.			X
Kannemeyer C.W.			X
Leeson F.J.			X
Mastus R.H.			X
Schultz W.C.			X
Whitty J.T.			X
Zeeman C.			X

DIAMOND FIELDS HORSE.

		Ba	Tr	Be
Maj.	Maxwell T.	X		
Cap./Adj.				
	Brand E.C.J.			X
Cap.Paym.				
	Ettling G.A.		X	
Capt.	Crause P.B.			X
	Lucas J.T.			X
	Rodger T.H. DSO			X
Lt.	Bodley J.H.			X
	Cramp R.S.			X
	Luxon T.H.			X
	Masterson M.H.			X
	Shackleton C.C.			X
	Ternent M.			X
Rsm.	Hough W.V.C.		X	
T/Sm.	Devenish F.A.K.			X
Trumpet Major.				
	Thwaites A.H.			X
Farr. Qms.				
	Needham G.R.			X
Arm.Sgt.				
	Crumplin A.			X

DIAMOND FIELDS HORSE Contd.

		Ba	Tr	Be
Saddler Sgt.				
	Freeman J.T.			X
Signaller Sgt.				
	Davie R.T.			X
Sgt.	Braine W.			X
	Cameron F.			X
	Donohoe J.	X		
	Hunter A.J.			X
	Martin A.H.			X
	Martin F.			X
	Mc Kerrow A.			X
	Milligan J.A.	X		
	Payne J.L.			X
	Watkins G.E.			X
	Whale H.			X
Cpl.	Barrett A.			X
	Blagden L.C.			X
	Cowen M.			X
	Edwards R.E.			X
	Griffin M.			X
	Hemsworth H.			X
	Woodruff C.			X
Trumpeter.				
	Croft H.M.			X
	Dickens E.D.			X
Pte./ Tpr.	Atkinson G.			X
	Beath F.T.			X
	Beeman T.J.			X
	Bevan J.			X
	Bishop R.J.			X
	Blakemore D.H.			X
	Brand E.			X
	Bredenkamp M.J.			X
	Brooklyn J.			X
	Brown C.H.			X
	Brown J.			X
	Brown J.H.			X
	Burnell P.			X
	Carlos J.F.			X
	Carnell H.			X

DIAMOND FIELDS HORSE Contd.

		Clasps		
		Ba	Tr	Be
Pte./ Tpr.	Carr J.P.			X
	Carson W.F.			X
	Cawood J.E.			X
	Chalmbers A.J.			X
	Chapman G.E.			X
	Colquhoun A.N.			X
	Connolly J.			X
	Cross H.T.			X
	Cuthbertson J.W.			X
	Dale A.M.			X
	Davies F.A.			X
	Davies T.F.			X
	de Villiers P.J.			X
	Donaldson A.McD.			X
	Druce J.C.			X
	Dyer J.R.			X
	Edgerton W.C.H.			X
	Evans R.			X
	Fisher H.	X		
	Forster E.D.			X
	Fry H.W.			X
	Gillingwater W.			X
	Glanville T.G.			X
	Hayes R.P.			X
	Heffer C.			X
	Heseltine E.W.			X
	Irvine H.A.S.			X
	Jackson G.W.			X
	Jacobs D.S.H.			X
	Jesson T.			X
	Jewell S.J.			X
	Jobson R.C.			X
	Johnson A.	X	X	
	Kellsey A.		..	X
	Kerr E.			X
	Kilroe G.R.			X
	King J.A.			X
	Knox F.H.			X
	Lawrence D.N.			X
	Lawson L.P.			X
	Lee G.T.H.			X
	Lewis P.P.			X
	Lopes G.S.			X
	Lorimer J.N.			X
	Mc Gregor E.R.			X
	Mc Kenna J.D.			X
	Mc Sheehy T.F.W.			X
	Mundell R.A.			X
	Nettman H.W.F.	X		
	Nolan T.			X
	O'Connor J.M.			X
	Parkin F.G.			X

DIAMOND FIELDS HORSE Contd.

		Clasps		
		Ba	Tr	Be
Pte./ Tpr.	Peters W.J.			X
	Plasket E.R.			X
	Poole A.W.			X
	Powell J.M.			X
	Pritchard M.J.			X
	Ralph E.			X
	Rand F.			X
	Rattham H.			X
	Ross G.W.			X
	Sadler J.M.			X
	Saunders R.			X
	Scott J.			X
	Sefton T.E.			X
	Shepherd W.F.			X
	Sheppy E.F.			X
	Sicklen F.W.			X
	Stewart W.M.			X
	Stuchbury A.G.			X
	Thom D.T.			X
	Townshend W.			X
	V/d Gryp F.			X
	V/d Walt G.H.			X
	Von Witt J.T.			X
	Walton R.		X	
	Watcham J.H.			X
	Watson J.H.			X
	White T.F.			X
	Wills H.J.			X
	Worrell W.H.			X
	Wustman F.R.			X

DICK'S KAFFRARIAN LEVIES

Also listed as
DICKS NATIVE LEVIES
DICKS LEVIES

		Ba	Tr	Be
Capt.	Hastings E.S.	X		
	Hickey C.H.	X		
	Hood D.J.	X		
	Johns S.E.	X	X	
	Mayberry W	X	X	
Lt.	Bundy T.D.	X		
	Smith A. St.L.	X	X	

		Clasps		
		Ba	Tr	Be
DUKES OF EDINBURGH'S OWN VOL. RIFLES.				
Commandant.				
	Frost J.		X	
Maj.	Daniells H.G.	X		
	Lewis J.			X
Capt./Adj.	Whindus E.J.	X		
Capt. Paym.	Dickson C.A.	X		
Capt.	Borchard C.P.			X
	Brown C.C.H.			X
	Charnock F.			X
	Hardey S.	X		
	Harker A.S.			X
	Johnson F.			X
	Mills K.J.			X
	Murison J.	X		
	Pennell F.M.S.			X
	Tennant H.	X		
Lt.Qm	Breakey J.	X		
Lt.	Barry J.	X		
	de Havilland T.L.			X
	Furniss O.	X		
	Malley H. St. C.			X
	May T.J.			X
	Pillans C.E.	X		
	Pillans R.	X	X	X
	Punnett H.R.			X
	Scholtz N.J.	X		
	Spence A.L.E.			X
	Stevens C.M.	X		
	Vance R.H.C.			X
Rsm.	Mc Quade J.F.	X		
S/M.	Tucker J.W.			X
Csm.	Dempsey P.			X
	Haycock H.J.			X
	Hellawell A.			X
Qms.	Curle J.P.			X
	Stapleton E.	X		

		Clasps		
		Ba	Tr	Be
DUKE OF EDINBURGH'S OWN VOL. RIFLES Contd.				
Sgt.	Bolton T.		X	
Sig. Sgt.	Bond W.H.			X
Sgt.	Broad B.			X
Bugle Sgt.	Camp C.R.			X
	Camp R.C.			X
	Coughlan M.V.	X		
Hosp. Sgt.	de Millac T.	X		
Sgt.	Dunn H.W.			X
	Fenix A.	X		
Saddler Sgt.				
	Fraser A.			X
Sgt.	Golden W.			X
	Goldsmid N.			X
	Goodison C.G.	X		
Paym. Sgt.	Gregory W.F.			X
Sgt.	Grist P.	X		
	Haigh W.	?	?	?
	Hastings G.			X
	Janisch N.	X		
	Johnson E.A.	X	X	
	Lee W.P.	X		
	Le Roux G.	X		
	Levitt S.E.	X		
	Mitchell P.			X
	Nichol J.			X
	Orchard J.H.	X		
	Ponton A.			X
	Rudolph C.J.			X
	Thompson W.W.	X		
	Viney J.			X
	Wakefield J.J.			X
	Williams C.D.			X
Farr.Sgt.				
	Williams J. (7th Dragoon Guards)			X

DUKE OF EDINBURGH'S OWN VOL. RIFLES Contd.

Rank	Name	Ba	Tr	Be
Sgt.	Wright A.J.			X
Cpl.	Abrahams H.N.		X	
	Barrett W.H.	X		
	Clark G.C.S.	X		
	Coetzee H.J.			X
	Collins E.			X
	Crighton D.J.			X
	Crole A.W.	X		
	Dunne F.			X
	Forster J.			X
	Gracie A.	X		
	Greetham H.F.J.	X		
	Hackett M.J.A.	X		
	Henderson J.C.			X
	Huckell J.			X
	Mann G.G.	X		
Sig. Cpl.	Mc Carthy I.			X
Cpl.	Mc Gillivray R.			X
	Power T.			X
	Rogerson J.R.			X
	Ross A.W.	X		
	Rowe C.F.			X
	Rudolph W.			X
	Sheppard A.			X
	Thurburn T.V.	X		
	Tonkin J.M.	X		
	Wadeley T.			X
	Wood P.J.			X
L/Cpl.	Bovell W.L.	X		
	Camp H.J.	X		
	Clark L.W.	X		
	Clark W.			X
	Cole W.C.	X		
	Coughlan W.J.	X		
	Gargan T.W.			X
	Halling J.F.			X
	Hardick D.	X		
	Robinson J.R.			X
	Rodwell T.	X	X	X
	Smeeton J.			X
	Stoffberg W.			X
	Thomas E.A.	X		
	Thomas J.R.	X		
Bugler.	Camp W.			X
	Fogarty A.			X

DUKE OF EDINBURGH'S OWN VOL. RIFLES Contd.

Rank	Name	Ba	Tr	Be
Bugler.	Jearey A.M.			X
	Long J.B.S.	X		
	Muller S.			X
	Williams H.			X
Drummer.	Farrell I.			X
	Farrell M.G.			X
	Reid P.			X
Pte./Tpr.	Adrianzen J.H.	X		
	Albertyn C.			X
	Allen H.M.	X		
	Allen J.C.			X
	Alt A.			X
	Anderson P.	X		
	Arends C.	X		
	Armer I.R.			X
	Art H.J.	X		
	Art J.	X		
	Atkinson A.			X
	Baasch W.	X		
	Bachforth T.	X		
	Baily P.			X
	Baker J.	X		
	Barry T.F.	X		
	Bartwick E.	X		
	Beckham G.	X		
	Bennett A.			X
	Bickell R.J.			X
	Bloomfield W.O.	X		
	Blows J.H.M.			X
	Bobbins J.G.			X
	Bolton J.			X
	Bowser G.			X
	Bowden B.H.	X		
	Brayshaw W.			X
	Breakey D.B.W.			X
	Bree D.P.			X
	Brevis W.J.	X		X
	Bridger W.M.			X
	Brooks W.			X
	Brown J.			X
	Browne F.			X
	Brown F.T.			X
	Bruce S.			X
	Brycie E.	X		
	Buckley M.			X
	Bunn D.			X
	Burn J.			X
	Buttenshaw G.	X		

DUKE OF EDINBURGH'S OWN VOL. RIFLES Contd.

Pte. Tpr.	Ba	Tr	Be
Byl E.A.	X		
Calmeyer J.	X		
Campbell R.			X
Carr J.	X		
Carr L.M.			X
Carter F.J.			X
Chartres W.G.	X		
Cheatter J.			X
Clegg C.F.	X		
Coetzee F.W.			X
Colling W.M.	X		
Collins J.	X		
Combrinck A.			X
Combrink H.N.	X		
Combrinck R.			X
Cooper J.H.			X
Cousins H.	X		
Coyne J.			X
Crole C.F.	X		
Curling C.			X
Cuthbertson J.W.			X
Cutting H.M.			X
Cruywagen J.J.			X
Dalrymple J.			X
Damon W.T.	X		
Danielz W.J.	X		
Davies J.R.	X		
Dekenah R.	X	X	
de la Haye F.			X
Delemere G.			X
Denyssen D.	X		
Deuchar A.M.	X		
De Vos W.	X		
Dickinson A.			X
Dorehill A.			X
Drew T.F.	X		
Driscoll J.			X
Drummond J.D.			X
Drysdale D.			X
Drysdale E.St. J.			X
Dufton W.	X		
Duncan J.			X
Duncan W.F.			X
Dunne F.J.			X
Dykman C.	X		
Dyson S.			X
Eager J.T.	X		
Eastwood P.B.	X		
Eayrs L.G.I.			X
Eayrs W.S.			X
Eayrs W.W.W.	X		

DUKE OF EDINBURGH'S OWN VOL. RIFLES Contd.

Pte. Tpr.	Ba	Tr	Be
Ebden J.	X		
Elliott G.			X
Elliott S.A.			X
Eustace R.K.	X		
Ferguson J.	X		
Finck L.			X
Fisher W.G.			X
Fletcher J.			X
Flisher G.T.	X		
Forbes A.W.	X		
Fortune S.P.	X		
Fowler R.G.	X		
Fox J.	X		
Gabriel G.S.	X		
Gain E.J.			X
Gersbach E.J.J.	X		
Giddey R.	X		
Gilpin J.			X
Gobart A.J.			X
Gold J.			X
Goodwin F.	X		
Grant F.K.			X
Gray A.			X
Green A.			X
Griggs H.J.	X		
Halling F.W.			X
Hanslo A.	X		
Hanson G.M.			X
Hargreaves W.			X
Harley T.			X
Hatton W.			X
Hayes W.			X
Heaven E.J.	X		
Heckroodt B.			X
Hendrikz J.G.	X		
Henney M.			X
Herbert F.	X		
Hesse H.B.			X
Heydenrych R.J.	X		
Hills G.H.			X
Hills S.H.			X
Hodgson C.E.			X
Hogan P.			X
Hogan T.			X
Hollingworth W.			X
Holmes G.H.			X
Holt C.J.			X
Howes E.R.	X		
Hughes E. St. G.A.			X
Hughes P.R.			X

DUKE OF EDINBURGH'S OWN VOL. RIFLES Contd.

		Clasps		
		Ba	Tr	Be
Pte.	Hume A.W.			X
Tpr.	Jacobs H.			X
	Jarman W.F.	X		
	Johnson W.J.			X
	Kebble H.			X
	Kelly J.G.	X		
	Kemp F.J.			X
	Kenniford G.	X		X
	Kessell W.H.			X
	Kettle E.			X
	Kilian F.L.	X		
	Kilian G.P.	X		
	Kirsten A.	X		
	Kirsten L.P.	X		
	Knight C.F.	X		
	Lacock H.			X
	Laidley T.J.			X
	Laing P.			X
	Lamont D.			X
	Larkin C.E.	X		
	Laskey W.			X
	Lawton D.R.	X		
	Lawton T.E.	X		
	Leary F.	X		
	Leary S.J.	X		
	Ledwith B.W.			X
	Lesar G.W.	X		
	Lexow A.L.C.	X	X	
	Litt H.E.	X		
	Logie C.W.	X		
	Longworth F.L.			X
	Mann W.F.			X
	Marquard W.W.	X		
	Marz W.B.			X
	Matthews J.A.	X		
	Mc Coy P.J.	X		
	Mc Donnell J.			X
	Mc Dowell J.	X		
	Mc Evay P.J.			X
	Mc Evoy T.	X		
	Mc Garry J.			X
	Mc Gowan P.			X
	Mc Grath J.			X
	Mc Leary G.	X		X
	Mc Leod A.H.	X	X	
	Mc Mahon J.			X
	Mc Millan B.	X		
	Mc Vitty W.			X
	Mello H.D.			X
	Millar W.	X		
	Miller G.	X		
	Mitchell W.		Tr	X

DUKE OF EDINBURGH'S OWN VOL. RIFLES Contd.

		Clasps		
		Ba	Tr	Be
Pte.	Moore D.H.			X
Tpr.	Mostert W.C.			X X
	Murphy M.			X
	Nagel G.J.			X
	Nicolays L.C.	X		
	Nielson D.			X
	O'Connor P.R.	X		
	O'Leary S.	X		
	Otto T.P.			X
	Owen W.J.			X
	Peake H.J.			X
	Pooley C.S.W.	X		
	Powell A.S.B.			X
	Preyser D.	X		
	Prideaux L.E.	X		
	Purcell R.B.	X		
	Quinn T.			X
	Reeks C.W.			X
	Rees H.	X		
	Rendell A.H.			X
	Reynierse H.P.			X
	Reynolds J.R.	X		
	Richards T.	X		
	Ridgway J.H.	X		
	Rienbach A.J.	X		
	Robb W.C.	X		
	Robertson G.D.L.	X		
	Robertson J.			X
	Robinson J.R.			X
	Rockley G.V.	X		
	Rodwell C.	X		
	Roscoe J.	X		
	Rose H.			X
	Rose W.			X
	Ross M.			X
	Ross T.G.			X
	Rothwell F.W.			X
	Russell C.B.	X		
	Russell G.	X		
	Rutgers A.A.	X		
	Rutherford L.	X		
	Sampson I.A.	X		
	Sandford S.J.	X		
	Sass J.			X
	Seaward P.H.			X
	Sharp W.	X		
	Sherry P.F.	X		
	Sims J.	X		
	Slabber T.C.	X		
	Smelton S.			X
	Smith A.W.	X		
	Smith E.G.	?	?	?

DUKE OF EDINBURGS OWN VOL RIFLES. Contd.

		Clasps		
		Ba	Tr	Be
Pte./Tpr.	Smith F.	X		
	Smith G.H.	X		
	Smith H.	X		
	Smith H.H.G.			X
	Smith J.	X	X	
	Smithdorf J.	X		X
	Smuts H.	X		
	Sparks G.F.	X		
	Sproul J.			X
	Spry W.M.			X
	Stanley J.T.			X
	Steel R.D.			X
	Stegmann P.U.	X		
	Stenhouse A.	X		
	Store F.	X		
	Stouffers H.	X		
	Stuart D.			X
	Swinnerton A.			X
	Takes F.J.			X
	Taplin C.	X		
	Taylor A.	X		
	Taylor C.H.			X
	Taylor E.			X
	Thomas E.A.			X
	Thompson A.D.			X
	Thompson J.			X
	Tittleton G.			X
	Tittleton W.			X
	Tomlinson J.	X		
	Tucker B.C.			X
	Tucker S.N.			X
	Tutt W.B.	X		
	Tytherleigh H.S.			X
	Uffindell A.B.			X
	Van Coller P.J.	X		
	Van der Spey B.			X
	Van Dyk A.	X		
	Van Eyk W.D.	X		
	Van Reenan M.			X
	Venner G.A.	X		
	Viljoen J.	X		
	Voget H.			X
	Voget R.F.			X
	Vos D.			X
	Waalster M.			X
	Waizel C.	X		
	Walder C.	X		
	Walton H.O.			X

DUKE OF EDINBURGS OWN VOL. RIFLES Contd.

		Clasps		
		Ba	Tr	Be
Pte./Tpr.	Ward F.			X
	Wardle W.S.J.			X
	Welff J.L.	X		
	Weisner P.			X
	Wells C.D.	X		
	Whatley H.			X
	White A.V.			X
	Whitwell H.			X
	Whittington G.			X
	Whitworth H.			X
	Whybrow F.W.			X
	Wiehahn C.			X
	Wrankmore R.	X		
	Wright L.			X
	Yallop H.	X		
	Yates A.W.			X

DYMES RIFLES Also listed as DIMES RIFLES

		Ba	Tr	Be
Lt.	Battye C.E.A.T.T.	X		
Sgt./Maj.	Kennedy J.D.	X		
	Peace G.	X		
	Shalvey P.J.	X		
Qms.	Laskey F.J.	X		X
Cpl.	Lewis S.J.	X		
Pte.	Ackerberg W.	X		X
	Ashwell J.	X		
	Bailey W.H.	X		
	Bains J.	X		
	Barrish H.P.R.M.	X		
	Brown Geo.	X		
	Brown J.	X		
	Clark W.	X		X
	Denny J.	X		
	Ebden J.A.	X		
	Evans H.	X		
	Full W.	X		
	Getzen H.G.		X	
	Hartigan J.A.	X		
	Hayman H.	X		
	Kieswetter D.	X		
	Langford J.B.	X		

DYMES RIFLES Contd.

		Clasps		
		Ba	Tr	Be
Pte.	Lawrence J.M.	X		
	Leibrandt S.A.O.	X		
	Maple A.D.	X		
	Maple G.	X		
	Maple W.	X		
	Marrinus H.	X		
	Morrison J.	X		
	Nickalls A.W.	X		
	Oakley E.R.	X		
	Scholtz W.G.A.	X		
	Scott T.E.	X		
	Skuse J.C.	X		
	Smith A.P.	X		
	Thomas D.J.	X		
	van de Hoeren N.J.	X	X	
	Woolward H.	X		

EAST GRIQUALAND FORCES

		Ba	Tr	Be
Commandant.				
	Strachan D.	X		

EAST LONDON ARTILLERY

		Ba	Tr	Be
Sgt.	Murphy T.	X		

EAST LONDON VOLUNTEER INFANTRY. Also listed as E. LONDON VOLS.

		Ba	Tr	Be
Lt.	Childe E.	X	X	
Tpr./ Pte.	Kirchoff A.W.	X	X	
	Mc Loughlin H.	X	X	
	Standing J.		X	

FERREIRAS HORSE.

		Ba	Tr	Be
Tpr./ Pte.	Donelly C.O.C.	X		
	Hayes E.J.	X	X	
	Mac Kniel E.	X		
	Scott J.W. (Also listed as Scott W.J.)	X		

FIELD FORCE.

		Ba	Tr	Be
Chaplain.				
	Cotton H.	X		

FIELD FORCE Contd.

		Ba	Tr	Be
Capt.	O'Toole J.	X		

FINGO LEVIES

		Ba	Tr	Be
Tpr.	Kali	X		X

FINGO SCOUTS.

		Ba	Tr	Be
Capt.	Green E.		X	

FINGO VOLUNTEERS.

		Ba	Tr	Be
Lt.	Anderson F.		X	

FIRST CITY VOLUNTEERS
Also listed as First City Mounted Volunteers 1st City Grahamstown Volunteers.

		Ba	Tr	Be
Maj.	Tamplin H.T.			X
Capt.	Sampson D.	X		
	Saunders F.A.			X
Lt.	Booth E.G.			X
	Galpin W.H.	X		
	Gowie C.	X		
	Grant P.F.			X
	Guest H.B.	X		
	Jeanes W.A.			X
	Lang-Sims J.H.			X
	Tillard R.	X		
	Wood S.W.	X		
Sgt./ Maj.	Hardacre T.	X		
	Jardine A.S.			X
	Noakes A.		X	X
	Street G.S.			X
Qms.	Gilder W.H.			X
	Kay W.			X
Col./ Sgt.	Grady J.	X		
Sgt.	Baker E.C.K.			X
	Bright W.	X		
	Capstick H.B.			X
	Eason C.C.			X
	Hutchinson T.F.	X		

FIRST CITY VOLUNTEERS contd.		Clasps		
		Ba	Tr	Be
Sgt.	Pitt J.	X		
	Quirk D.	X		
Band Sgt.	Rogers J.O.	X		
Sgt.	Rogers W.H.		X	
	Street H.		X	
	Wallace F.N.	X		
	Wilks W.S.	X		
	Winstanley G.	X		
	Winter E.T.	X		
	Winter J.P.	X		
	Woolard A.		X	
Cpl.	Derecourt T.W.	X		
	Edwards C.L.		X	
	Fawcett J.A.		X	
	Fielding W.	X		
	Gush J.M.		X	
	Hall J.D.		X	
	Harper L.J.J.		X	
	Lloyd L.O.	X		
	Long E.		X	
Cpl./ Bugler.	Orsmond J.		X	
Cpl.	Phillamore G.H.		X	
	Porter D.H.	X		
	Sampson J.C.	X		
	Van der An F.	X		
	Whiteside J.P.		X	
L/Cpl.	Reed H.R.		X	
Pte./ Tpr.	Adams F.	X		
	Arrow A.H.		X	
Bugler.	Ashington S.M.		X	
Pte./ Tpr.	Avery W.	X		
	Baker G.J.		X	
	Barnsley W.A.	X		
	Bartle G.	X		
	Bertram H.L.	X		
	Bishop J.M.	X		

FIRST CITY VOLUNTEERS Contd.		Clasps		
		Ba	Tr	Be
Pte./ Tpr.	Blake A.J.	X		
	Botten C.R.A.			X
	Boucher G.H.	X		
	Bowles R.G.			X
	Brooks W.H.	X		
	Bunce J.	X		
	Burgess A.			X
	Burgess W.R.			X
	Butt C.			X
	Cairns H.L.			X
	Campbell R.J.	X		X
	Chapman W.J.			X
	Cinnamon I.	X		
	Cinnamon W.G.	X		
	Coleman J.			X
	Coure G.			X
	Cowie G.			X
	Dickason A.E.			X
	Dickason F.A.			X
	Dickens E.E.			X
	Duggan E.J.	X		
	Elenton H.C.			X
	Emslie A.C.N.			X
	Emslie P.W.			X
	Fairbridge W.E.	X		
	Farndell W.	X		X
	Fisher A.C.			X
	Fletcher R.A.	X		
	Fray A.	X		X
	Gill H.	X		X
	Goldschmidt J.	X		
	Goodwin W.H.	X		
	Gradidge W.C.	X		
	Grady E.J.			X
	Grady J.	X		
	Green W.A.	X		
	Gush G.A.			X
	Hackart C.			X
	Hambridge T.R.	X		
	Harris W.S.			X
	Hayes P.C.			X
	Hayter T.S.			X
	Hodgkinson J.A.	X		
	Hoggan W.	X		
	Hope W.H.A.			X
	Hutchinson S.	X		
	Jamieson J.	X		
	Jeanes E.			X
	Jeanes N.J.			X

FIRST CITY VOLUNTEERS. Contd.

Rank	Name	Ba	Tr	Be
Pte./Tpr.	Jefferys J.F.			X
	Jennings J.E.	X	X	
	Johnson J.W.			X
	Jonson E.			X
	Jordan T.M.			X
	Kemp W.	X		X
	Lachimdt L.	X		
	Langley E.J.	X		
	Levy E.B.	X		
	Lloyd M.E.			X
	Lloyd W.E.			X
	Logie W.			X
	Long J.J.			X
	Long P.S.			X
	Long R.A.			X
	Lynn J.	X		X
	Marsden A.E.	X		X
	Mc Cann W.W.F.			X
	Mc Leod A.	X		
	Mills W.H.			X
	Moore A.			X
	Moore R.			X
	Mosworthy F.T.			X
	Mould W.J.			X
	Murray E.J.			X
	Olyott J.W.			X
	Openshaw D.	X		X
	Orsmond L.C.			X
	Parfitt G.	X		
	Parsons T.		X	X
	Petersen D.			X
Bugler.	Praed F.A.			X
Pte./Tpr.	Preston J.J.			X
	Priest D.H.			X
	Roe H.			X
	Roe H.J.			X
	Roe W.			X
	Rutherford F.			X
	Shaw G.C.	X		
	Smith H.J.			X
	Smith R.			X
	Smith W.H.	X		
	Stewart A.	X		
	Stewart Alex	X		
	Strutt E.W.G.			X
	Sundquest E.			X
	Tribe W.C.			X
	Van der An F.C.			X
	Vroom W.H.			X

FIRST CITY VOLUNTEERS. Contd.

Rank	Name	Ba	Tr	Be
Bugler.				
	Wakeford A.B.	X		
Pte./Tpr.	Watkins C.			X
	Webber G.A.			X
	Webber J.			X
	Webber W.J.	X		
	Webbstock H.J.			X
Bugler.	Weineck L.G.			
Pte./Tpr.	Westaway L.B.			X
	Whitehorn F.W.			X
	Williams H.E.			X
	Williams J.	X		
	Wood W.T.	X		

FORT BEAUFORT VOLUNTEERS

Rank	Name	Ba	Tr	Be
Pte.	Pedlar G.H.	X		

FORT WHITE VOLUNTEERS

Rank	Name	Ba	Tr	Be
Bugler.	Kilduff T.	X		

F.A.M. POLICE (Frontier Armed & Mtd. Police)

Rank	Name	Ba	Tr	Be
Pte.	Jones J.O.	X		
	Thompson C.D.	X		

FRONTIER CARBINEERS.

Also listed as Frontier Carabineers.

Rank	Name	Ba	Tr	Be
Lt.	Head H.F.		X	
	Wright J.I.		X	
Tpr./Pte.	Allen J.		X	
	Clarke E.D.		X	
	Curtis G.		X	X
	Hadley H.		X	
	Rusch A.		X	
	Rusch E.		X	
	Wall E.M.		X	
	White P.F.	X	X	

FROSTS COLUMN.

Rank	Name	Ba	Tr	Be
Capt./Adj.	Cumming W.G.		X	

		Clasps		
		Ba	Tr	Be

FROSTS COLUMN Contd.

Rank	Name	Ba	Tr	Be
Lt.	Ross H.D.C. (Staff Off.)		X	

GELUK MOUNTED VOLUNTEERS

Rank	Name	Ba	Tr	Be
Tpr.	Streak R.C.			X

GENERAL CLARKES STAFF. Also listed as Staff of Gen. Clarke.

Rank	Name	Ba	Tr	Be
Capt.	Gibbs T.F.	X		
Sgt.	Lee W.D.	X		

General Service.

Rank	Name	Ba	Tr	Be
No Rank.	Cowper S.	X		

GEORGE BURGHERS Also listed as George Town Burghers / George Volunteers

Rank	Name	Ba	Tr	Be
Capt.	Ferreira S.M.		X	
Lt.	Bell E.	X	X	
	Scotland T.J.		X	
Qms.	Mills E.J.H.		X	
Sgt.	Coppens J.G.		X	
	Holtzkamf C.J.		X	
	Ollett R.R.		X	
Pte.	Aspeling E.L.		X	
	Benn W.J.		X	
Tpr.	Brown P.		X	
	Murdoch J.	X	X	
	Thorpe L.		X	
	Whatley W.H.		X	

GONUBIE HORSE. Also listed as GNUBIE M. RIFLES. GONUBIE Mtd. VOL.

Rank	Name	Ba	Tr	Be
Sgt./Maj.	Bousfield F.H.		X	

GONUBIE HORSE Also listed as GNUBIE M. RIFLES. **GONUBIE MTD. VOL. Contd.**

Rank	Name	Ba	Tr	Be
Pte.	Delange W.J.		X	
	Milford T.	X	X	
	Muller C.J.		X	
	Nel R.J.J.		X	
	van Rensburg H.G.		X	
	van Rensburg H.J.		X	
	van Rensburg J.		X	
	Warren W.		X	
	Wulff C.S.		X	

GORDONIA VOLUNTEERS.

Rank	Name	Ba	Tr	Be
Capt.	Will J.H.N.			X
Lt.	Blane F.T.			X
Sgt./Maj.	Will F.G.			X
Qms.	Panizza L.G.			X
Sgt.	Holmes O.			X
	Scholtz C.F.			X
	Scott W.			X
	Watson C.F.			X
Cpl.	Brink J.			X
	Dick S.			X
	Diergaardt W.			X
	Domingo J.			X
	Herborn W.			X
	Steeneveldt J.			X
	Theron G.			X
Tpr.	Bassow G.			X
	Beukes D.		X	X
	Beukes G.			X
	Beukes G.			X
	Beukes J.			X
	Beukes P.			X
	Botha J.J.			X
	Cloete D.			X
	Coetzee A.			X
	Coetzee D.			X
	Daniels F.			X
	de Juy F.			X
	De Klerk B.			X
	De Wet J.			X

GORDONIA VOLUNTEERS.

		Clasps		
		Ba	Tr	Be
Tpr.	Diergaardt G.			X
	Domingo P.			X
	Eiman N.			X
	Esterhuizen W.			X
	Ezau G.			X
	Farmer P.			X
	Feris W.			X
	Frank C.			X
	Hollembach P.			X
	Isaacs F.			X
	Isaacs N.			X
	Jannetjes F.J.			X
	Jansen C.			X
	Jansen D.			X
	Klaaste C.			X
	Klaaste S.			X
	Klazen W.			X
	Kolff R. v. D.			X
	Koopman W.			X
	Kotzee J.			X
	Losper H.			X
	Louw N.			X
	Maasdorp J.			X
	Manton R.			X
	Markham R.			X
	Mc Dougall P.R.			X
	Nel J.			X
	Nel M.			X
	Pretorius C.			X
	Rose J.			X
	Rose W.			X
	Saail F.			X
	Schalkwyk J.			X
	September A.			X
	Sneyer A.			X
	Stevens J.			X
	Theron N.H.			X
	Titis G.			X
	Thys D.			X
	van der Colff			X
	van Rooi F.			X
	van Wyk A.D.			X
	van Wyk C.			X
	van Wyk H.			X
	Visagie W.			X
	Willems A.			X
	Witbooi W.F.			X

GRAAFF REINET BURGHERS.

		Ba	Tr	Be
Capt.	Marriott H.H.		X	
	Minnaar H.J.		X	

GRAAFF REINET BURGHERS. Contd.

		Ba	Tr	Be
Lt.	Connor J.A.		X	
	Hind G.		X	
	Minnaar H.J. (Jnr.)		X	
Sgt./Maj.	Hulzer H.J.W.		X	
Qms.	Fick J.J.		X	
	Smuts C.W.		X	
Sgt.	Brummer D.	X	X	
	Waldeck J.J.		X	
Cpl.	Mansfield E.		X	
	Mc Bride J.J.	X	X	
	Naude D.F.	X	X	
Pte./Tpr.	Barnes A.H.		X	
	Enslin G.F.		X	
	Enslin H.A.		X	
	Gibbs A.		X	
	Greeff J.H.		X	
	Haarhoff N.F.		X	
	Jansen R.A.	X	X	
	Keane J.C.		X	
	Martins W.J.		X	
	Mc Cusker T.		X	
	Murray F.		X	
	Robinson C.		X	
	Swanepoel J.F.		X	
	Victor S.J.	X		

GRAAFF REINET ROVERS.

		Ba	Tr	Be
Capt.	Boshoff H.G.	X	X	
Pte./Tpr.	Foster F.	X	X	
	Leech G.F.	X	X	
	Loggerenberg J.	X	X	

GRAHAMSTOWN MOUNTED INFANTRY.

		Ba	Tr	Be
Tpr.	Millar H.C.			X

GRAHAMSTOWN VOL. H. ARTILLERY Also listed as GRAHAMSTOWN HORSE ARTY.

		Ba	Tr	Be
Capt.	Nelson A.E.	X		

GRAHAMSTOWN VOL. H. ARTILLERY. Also listed as GRAHAMSTOWN HORSE ARTY.

Rank	Name	Ba	Tr	Be
Sgt./Maj.	Jamieson J.J.	X		
	Mc Intosh J.C.	X		
Qms.	Hinton W.H.	X		
Sgt.	Orren F.E.	X		
Bomb.	Will W.H.		X	
Gnr.	Clark T.	X		
	Eaton G.	X		
	Edwards G.T.J.	X	X	
	Hartwell J.F.	X		
	Juby J.W.	X		
	Meyer C.	X	X	
Driver	Norton W.S.	X		
Gnr.	Wood M.J.	X		

GRAYS GONUBIE VOLUNTEERS Also listed as GRAYS G.M. VOLS.

Rank	Name	Ba	Tr	Be
Sgt.	Zeller J.		X	
Tpr./Pte.	Nicholson C.E.		X	
	Nicholson J.H.		X	
	Rennie A.D.		X	
	Zeller J.R.		X	

GRIQUALAND WEST BRIGADE

Rank	Name	Ba	Tr	Be
Commandant.	Green T.	X		
Lt.Col.	Harris D.			X
Lt.	Clark H.E.			X
	Stead B.			X
Guide & Intelligence Officer.	Field H.G.			X

GRIQUALAND WEST BRIGADE Contd.

Rank	Name	Ba	Tr	Be
Band Cpl.	Hayes W.			X
	Perdue W.J.			X
L/Cpl.	Leschinsk A.			X
Inf.Det.Pte.	Dicks H.J.			X
Bandsman.	Mc Kenzie W.N.			X
Pte.	Bonner A.G.			X
	Lenkwane T.D.P.			X

GRIQUALAND WEST NATIVE CONTINGENT.

Rank	Name	Ba	Tr	Be
Commandant.	Bailie A.C.	X		
Capt.	Savory C.R.	X		
Lt.	Nugent J.	X		
	Tayler J.A.E.		X	
	Wood J.	X		
Tpr.	Weale F.J.		X	

HAMPSHIRE ARTILLERY.

Rank	Name	Ba	Tr	Be
Lt.	Vizard A.	X	X	

HARVEYS HORSE.

Rank	Name	Ba	Tr	Be
Adjutant.	Marsh A.	X		
Capt.	Allen C.J.	X	X	
Lt.	Kinieys-Tynte A.M.P.		X	
Sgt.	Houghton W.R.		X	

HARVEYS HORSE.

Rank	Name	Ba	Tr	Be
Pte./	Gehring H.H.		X	
Tpr.	Holm A.P.L.		X	
	Holtzkampf J.B.		X	
	Keog W.		X	
	Neal R.P.		X	
	Walter C.		X	
	Warren A.		X	

HELVENS HORSE.

Rank	Name	Ba	Tr	Be
Cpl.	Marriott G.		X	

HERSCHEL NATIVE CONTINGENT.

Rank	Name	Ba	Tr	Be
Commandant.	Hook D.B.	X	X	
Capt.	Harrison L.M.	X		
	Impey R.P.	X		
	Kayser M.K.C.	X	X	
	Perks T.	X		
	Stevens H.	X		
Lt.	Adams T.	X		
	Hall F.G.	X		
	Hillier H.A.	X	X	
	Kayser R.	X	X	
	Morris E.W.H.	X		
	Rieger J.C.E.	X		
	Schentke C.P.	X		
Sgt.	Parkie J.W.	X		

HOPETOWN BURGHERS.

Rank	Name	Ba	Tr	Be
Lt.	Wright J.W.	X		
Sgt.	Abbott C.	X		
Cpl.	Whitehead E.	X		
Pte./	Koen C.A.	X		
Tpr.	Myburgh W.	X		
	Smith F.	X		
	Van Wyk W.	X		

HUMANSDORP VOLUNTEERS.
Also listed as: HUMANSDORP BURGHERS.
HUMANSDORP LIGHT HORSE.

Rank	Name	Ba	Tr	Be
Cpl.	Wait R.P.		X	

HUMANSDORP VOLUNTEERS. Contd.

Rank	Name	Ba	Tr	Be
Tpr.	Chippert F.A.		X	

HUNTS VOLUNTEERS.

Rank	Name	Ba	Tr	Be
Lt.	Haw C.R.	X		
Sgt./Maj.	Crooks T.S.			X

IDUTYWA MILITIA.
Also listed as IDUTYWA LEVIES

Rank	Name	Ba	Tr	Be
Capt.	Godfrey W.P.		X	
Lt.	Mac Donald J.C.		X	

INTELLIGENCE.

Rank	Name	Ba	Tr	Be
Lt.	Miller T.G.A.			X
Sgt./Maj.	Smith R.A.L.			X
Sgt.	Miller F.M.			X
Pte.	Goss W.M. (also duplicated as Goss M.W.)		X	

IRREGULAR HORSE. Also known as NELTLETON IRREGULAR HORSE.

Rank	Name	Ba	Tr	Be
Lt.	Mainwaring E.C.L.T.	X		

JAMESTOWN VOLUNTEERS.

Rank	Name	Ba	Tr	Be
Sgt./Maj.	Anderson W.M.		X	

KAFFRARIAN LEVIES.

Rank	Name	Ba	Tr	Be
Commandant.	Dick R.J.	X		
Capt.	Warneford W.J.J.	X		
Lt.	Rayner C.F.	X		X

KAFFRARIAN RIFLES.

Rank	Name	Clasps Ba	Tr	Be
Capt./Adj.	Cumming H.B.			X
Surgeon Capt.	Darley-Hartley W.			X
Lt.	Maclean J.W.	X		X
	Wakefield C.D.			X
	Williams E.S.			X
Qms.	Currin R.W.			X
Csm.	Coleman R.			X
	Honan M.P.			X
Sgt.	Currin A.G.			X
	Dryburgh A.			X
	Hinks B.K.			X
	Knobel F.C.			X
	Nicholls H.M.			X
	Smith H.W.			X
Cpl.	Behr W.C.			X
	Braithwaite L.			X
	Dickerson F.T.			X
	Forsyth J.A.			X
	Maclean W.A.			X
Bug.Cpl.	Mc Lean L.			X
Cpl.	Nicholls B.C.W.			X
	Paget W.A.			X
	Potter F.H.			X
	Saunders C.R.			X
	Tinley E.			X
L/Cpl.	Geddie W.			X
	Harris E.L.			X
	Lloyd W.W.			X
	Wells J.		X	
	Wright W.		X	
Pte.	Anderson R.			X
	Andrews R.A.			X
	Bollman A.			X
	Brock A.			X
	Brown H.V.			X
	Burns G.			X
	Burns W.			X
	Cayton M.			X
	Chappell F.R.			X
	Cook H.			X

KAFFRARIAN RIFLES Contd.

Rank	Name	Clasps Ba	Tr	Be
Pte.	Critchfield R.			X
	Currin O.J.			X
	Davey A.E.			X
	Drewes G.			X
	Dryburgh A.T.			X
	Etherton J.			X
	Farrell H.A.			X
	Fox G.			X
	Geddie J.W.			X
	Goodyer F.H.			X
	Graham A.R.			X
	Greenwood W.H.			X
	Grenfell W.			X
	Hartley P.F.			X
	Hawkins W.R.			X
	Hooker E.L.			X
	Impey C.B.			X
	Johnston J.Mc D.			X
	Keeney F.			X
	Keeney F.W.			X
	Kellet E.			X
	Kelley P.P.			X
	Ketel R.		X	
	Laaks J.			X
	Lambart F.A.O.			X
	Lewis W.			X
	Lloyd C.A.			X
	Lloyd W.W.			X
	Mac Donald A.C.			X
	Mac Donald J.D.			X
	Martin N.F.			X
	Mc Innes A.			X
	Mc Loughan G.W.			X
	Metcalfe H.G.P.			X
	Morgan L.T.			X
	Muller C.W.			X
	Muller P.F.			X
	Nelson E.C.			X
	Ogilvie G.W.			X
	Reyniers A.			X
	Reyniers A.L.T.			X
	Reynolds G.			X
	Roux W.R.			X
	Slogrove J.J.			X
	Small B.			X
	Smith H.B.			X
	Stewart E.			X
	Westaway C.			X
	Wilson R.J.			X
	Wilson T.H.			X
	Wood J.H.		X	

KAFFRARIAN VOLUNTEER ARTILLERY.

Rank	Name	Ba	Tr	Be
Capt.	Nicolls C.E.	X		
Lt.	White W.J.	X		
Trumpet Major.				
	Lewis F.W.	X		
Sgt.	Bender E.	X		
	Grandin P.	X		
	Timmer J.	X		
Cpl.	Clear D.M.	X		
Pte./Gnr.	Bennett J.	X		
	Brady J.	X		
	Green R.	X	X	
	Horsley W.J.	X		
	Jefferson T.H.R.	X		
	Mellish J.	X		
	Mitchell R.	X	X	
	Morton F.J.	X		
	Murray A.G.	X		

KAMASTONE FINGOES.
Also listed as KAMASTONE LEVY. FINGO LEVIES KAMASTONE

Rank	Name	Ba	Tr	Be
Lt.	Cowie W.W.	X	X	
	Green H.E.O.	X	X	

KEISKAMA HOEK VOLUNTEERS

Rank	Name	Ba	Tr	Be
Sgt.	Bentz F.	X		
	Peter F.	X		
Cpl.	Frauenstein A.	X		
Tpr./Pte.	Ehlert C.	X		
	Humpel A.	X		
	Kietzman C.A.F.	X		
	Lewrentz C.	X		
	Schenk F.	X		
	Schroeder W.F.	X		

KIMBERLEY HORSE. Also listed as KIMBERLEY LIGHT HORSE.

Rank	Name	Ba	Tr	Be
Capt./Adj.	MacPherson E.D.	X		

KIMBERLEY HORSE. Also listed as KIMBERLEY LIGHT HORSE. Contd.

Rank	Name	Ba	Tr	Be
Capt.	Doyle G.C.	X		
	MacPherson W.P.G.	X		
Lt.	Chadwick E.H.	X		
	Day R.W.	X		
	Heath C.W.	X		
	Hutchinson G.W.	X		
	Mayers A.P.	X		
	Rickman W.E.	X		
	Tyler S.D.F.	X		
Sgt./Maj.	Art T.	X		
	Figg T.R.	X		
	Ireland A.	X		
	Whyte B.L.	X		
Sgt.	Coston H.J.	X		
	Floyd F.H.	X		
	Henty C.G.	X		
Trumpet Major.				
	Holmes R.	X		
Sgt.	Wilson L.	X		
Cpl.	Bolton M.	X		
	Clark F.R.	X		
	Fitzgerald J.	X		
	Mac Queen J.	X		
	Oliver W.E.	X		
	Tidmarsh T.	X		
Pte./Tpr.	Abbott F.T.	X		
	Bailey J.G.	X		
	Bennett J.	X		
	Bramsen C.W.	X		
	Brodrick M.	X		
	Brophy W.J.	X	X	
	Budge H.	X		
	Carver T.J.	X		
	Cole E.G.	X		
	Craig J.	X		
	Crickmay H.G.			X
	Crosbie W.		X	
	Delaney J.	X		
	Francis R.H.	X		
	Isacke J.L.	X		
	Jackson J.	X		
	Johnson G.			X
	Kennedy M.	X		
	Kennedy W.	X		
	Kerr H.J.	X		

KIMBERLEY HORSE. Also listed as KIMBERLEY LIGHT HORSE. Contd.

		Clasps		
		Ba	Tr	Be
Pte./ Tpr.	Ladyson W.E.	X		
	Marais P.	X		
	Mc Neil A.	X		
	Morey J.	X		
	Muller H.L.	X		
	Paterson J.	X		
	Peach G.	X		
	Petersen W.	X		
	Philpot H.	X		
	Ritchards J.P.H.	X		
	Ritchie T.	X		
	Rogers J.	X		
	Rose W.	X		
	Rush D.B.	X		X
	Sharp D.	X		
	Smith C.	X		
	Smith J.	X		
	Spadoni J.	X		
	Storm W.	X		
	Visser H.	X		
	Wilson J.	X		
	Wright E.			X

KIMBERLEY RIFLES. Also listed as KIMBERLEY REGIMENT. KIMBERLEY REG. VOLS.

		Ba	Tr	Be
Maj.	Finlayson R.A.			X
Capt.	Duirs M.			X
	Green A.J.			X
	Moseley E.H.			X
Lt.	Angel T.L.			X
	Bridge J.M.			X
	Howie C.			X
	Humphrys E.F.			X
	Muir A.D.J. (Kimberley Scots)			X
Vet.Lt.	Lindsay J.			X
Brig./Sm.				
	Mac Farlane D.K.			X
Rsm.	Tozer E.E.M.			X

KIMBERLEY RIFLES. Also listed as KIMBERLEY REGIMENT. KIMBERLEY REG. VOLS. Contd.

		Clasps		
		Ba	Tr	Be
Csm.	Devonshire W.T.			X
	Fyvie L.C.			X
	Mc Donald J.R.			X
	Ozard R.			X
	Selling W.G.			X
Pipe Maj.				
	Duncan W.G.			X
Sgt.	Banham W.C.			X
	Bristow S.A.			X
	Burton C.L.			X
	Cherry C.			X
	Church H.C.			X
	Cockrell F.			X
	Forsyth G.			X
	Harrison F.			X
	Hogg J.			X
	Horn F.			X
	Johnson J.W.			X
	Lawrence N.			X
	Matthews T.H.			X
	McKenzie R.J.			X
	Mc Knight T.J.			X
	Ozad R.			X
	Petrie J.			X
	Porter Mc L.			X
	Richards T.B.			X
	Stevenson J.			X
	Woodin G.			X
Cpl.	Bell J.			X
	Ferro F.W.			X
	Goldwyer H.			X
	Grant J.G.			X
	Hodgekinson W.J.			X
	Jones F. Owen			X
	Macpherson A.E.			X
	Mellville H.G.			X
	Ortner E.G.			X
	Parker G.			X
	Penn F.H.			X
	Preston G.			X
	Rugen A.J.			X
	Smith A.W.			X
	Stewart J.			X

KIMBERLEY RIFLES. Also listed as KIMBERLEY REGIMENT. KIMBERLEY REG. VOLS. Contd.

		Clasps		
		Ba	Tr	Be
Cpl.	Williams W.R.			X
	Wright G.F.			X
L/Cpl.	Ford T.J.			X
	Grieve P.C.			X
	Gwynn G.			X
	Jakins A.J.			X
Piper	Gallow A.H.			X
	Gibson G.			X
Bugler.	Dickinson A.F.			X
	Kennett G.T.			X
Drummer.	Wright J.L.			X
Pte.	Allen C.J.			X
	Archdale W.F.			X
	Armstrong J.			X
	Baldry W.C.			X
	Bartlett G.A.			X
	Bedgood A.F.			X
	Bishop R.			X
	Blassoples A.			X
	Boyd R.			X
	Brooks H.J.			X
	Carr H.J.			X
	Carter H.C.			X
	Charles J.			X
	Close P.T.S.			X
	Cole R.			X
	Cox W.E.			X
	Cumming J.A.			X
	De Melker A.G.			X
	Dennis A.			X
	Driver J. (Clasp Ba as shown in Roll)	X		
	Driver W.E.			X
	du Prat G.B.			X
	Dyer J.			X
	Ellis G.J.			X
	Fagan B.			X
	Ferro H.V.			X
	Fisher J.A.			X
	Fitzpatrick H.J.			X
	Fullaway H.R.			X
	George L.			X

KIMBERLEY RIFLES. Also listed as KIMBERLEY REGIMENT. KIMBERLEY REG. VOLS. Contd.

		Clasps		
		Ba	Tr	Be
Pte.	George L.F.			X
	Goldwyer W.			X
	Goodall A.W.			X
	Graham T.J.			X
	Haddock W.L.			X
	Hall S.E.			X
	Halley A.			X
	Ham T.P.			X
	Hamer H.			X
	Harper J.			X
	Harries I.C.			X
	Hendricks W.			X
	Hockey E.P.			X
	Holding F.J.			X
	Hurford T.G.			X
	Innes J.D.			X
	Jackson J.			X
	Jameson H.			X
	Johnson G.F.			X
	Kerr F.			X
	Knight C.J.			X
	Laing J.			X
	Langford A.J.			X
	Lawrence W.			X
	Leigh J.			X
	Lemon A.			X
	Lester D.W.			X
	Lezard H.E.S.			X
	Lezard L.F.			X
	Main J. (Listed as Kimberley Scouts)			X
	Main W.			X
	Maloney J.H.			X
	Masters G.			X
	Masters W.T.			X
	Mc Donald C.A.			X
	Mc Kay J.			X
	Mc Kenzie J.			X
	Mc Kenzie W.			X
	Mc Lachlan W.J.			X
	Mc Master D.J.A.			X
	Mellet T.B.			X
	Mitchell J.			X
	Mitchell W.C.			X
	Moult A.M.			X
	Norman T.R.			X
	Oldridge F.W.			X

KIMBERLEY RIFLES. Also listed as KIMBERLEY REGIMENT. KIMBERLEY REG. VOLS. Contd.

Rank	Name	Ba	Tr	Be
Pte.	Olifant T.			X
	Paterson A.			X
	Pimm R.H.			X
	Raaff T.H.			X
	Rae A.			X
	Rayner A.E.			X
	Rayner W.A.			X
	Rippington T.			X
	Robertson H.H.			X
	Robertson J.M.			X
	Robinson W.W.			X
Bandsm.	Rossiter W.G.			X
Pte.	Rowland A.C.			X
	Sadler W.			X
	Savage A.H.			X
	Savage P.J.			X
	Shimeld S.			X
	Skea A.D.			X
	Smith E.T.F.			X
	Smith T.W.			X
	Smith W.			X
	Steytler N.			X
	Stockwell E.H.			X
	Sullivan J.			X
	Sweet A.J.			X
	Taylor W.T.			X
	Timbrell R.M.			X
	Unkles A.P.			X
	Vaughan E.J.			X
	Wallis E.G.			X
	Walters J.J.			X
	Ward B.T.			X
	Ward F.R.			X
	Ward J.W.			X
	Wilcock A.G.H.			X
	Wilcock J.			X

KINGS ROYAL RIFLES THE 3RD

Rank	Name	Ba	Tr	Be
Sgt.	Birch B.H.		X	
	Crooke G.		X	
L/Sgt.	Clifton E.		X	
Pte.	Nixon F.		X	
	Palmer C.H.	X		
	Peacock J.T.	X		

KINGS ROYAL RIFLES THE 3RD Contd.

Rank	Name	Ba	Tr	Be
Pte.	Winehouse A.			X

KING WILLIAMS TOWN VOL. ARTILLERY.

Rank	Name	Ba	Tr	Be
Capt.	Dyer F.		X	
Lt.	Tremeer C.A.C.		X	
Qms.	Bate F.S.		X	
Gnr./Tpr.	Brauns A.D.		X	
	Collier A.W.		X	
Bugler.				
	Deary A.E.		X	
Gnr./Tpr.	Deary N.D.		X	
	Dobson R.		X	
	Lowry H.T.		X	
	Richmond J.E.		X	
	Young S.J.		X	

KNYSNA VOLUNTEERS.

Rank	Name	Ba	Tr	Be
Lt.	Blanck E.	X		

KOKSTAD MOUNTED VOLUNTEERS. Also listed as KOKSTAD MOUNTED RIFLES

Rank	Name	Ba	Tr	Be
Commandant.	Wylde J.T.	X	X	
Lt./Adj.	Matthews C.		X	
Lt.	Midgley E.		X	
	Uys B.	X	X	
Chaplin.	Dixon E.Y.		X	
Sgt./Maj.	Gordon H.A.		X	
Sgt.	Kelly E.	X		
	Neumeyer J.		X	
	Taylor A.		X	
	Warren F.J.	X		

KOKSTAD MOUNTED VOLUNTEERS Also listed as KOKSTAD MOUNTED RIFLES Contd.

Rank	Name	Ba	Tr	Be
Cpl.	Hirst A.L.	X	X	
L/Cpl.	Edwards T.		X	
Tpr./Pte.	Adam J.		X	
	Alleman F.D.R.		X	
	Barclay J.		X	
	Beuster K.H.M.	X	X	
	Davie J.		X	
	Dorkin R.J.B.	X	X	
	Gorman T.E.S.	X	X	
	Kok W.J.	X	X	
	Macefield W.	X	X	
	Slaughter J.M.		X	
	Spencer T.F.		X	
	Yeatman T.		X	

KOMGHA MOUNTED VOLUNTEERS. Also listed as KOMGHA BURGHERS.

Rank	Name	Ba	Tr	Be
Cpl.	Gunn W.C.		X	
Tpr.	Taylor H.S.		X	

LADY FRERE NATIVE LEVY. Also listed as LADY FRERE LEVY.

Rank	Name	Ba	Tr	Be
Lt.	Bands E.		X	

LANDREYS LIGHT HORSE. Also listed as LANDREYS HORSE.

Rank	Name	Ba	Tr	Be
Commandant.	Landrey J.	X	X	
Capt.	Evans E.J.	X	X	
	Roome H.A.	X	X	
	Stourton A.J.	X		
Lt.	Chilman H.R.	X		
	Clark H.J.		X	
	Ellis G.K.	X		
	King C.A.	X		

LANDREYS LIGHT HORSE. Also listed as LANDREYS HORSE.

Rank	Name	Ba	Tr	Be
Lt.	Landrey F.W.	X		
	Munro H.T.	X		
Rsm.	Hewitt C.	X		
S/M.	Marsh C.S.	X	X	X
	Murray L.J.	X	X	
Qms.	Smith W.H.	X	X	
Sgt.	Beeton R.	X		
	Dilley C.		X	
	East E.	X		
	Gloyne H.	X	X	
	Harvey H.	X		
	Morrison L.	X		
	Thiel F.	X	X	
	Tibbetts E.J.	X		
Cpl.	Carrihill T.	X		
	Chester G.		X	
	Ellis A.F.	X		
	Ellis R.	X	X	
	Jacobz J.A.	X	X	
	Pinnoy J.W.	X	X	
	Rice J.	X		
Tpr.	Abrahams J.	X		
	Bayley P.C.	X		
	Bentley E.W.		X	
	Bentley J.	X	X	
	Birch J.E.		X	
	Boxall E.J.		X	
	Byron T.	X		
	Campbell A.A.	X		
	Campbell E.	X		
	Campbell W.	X		
	Draai P.N.	X		
	Duke T.		X	
	Dunn R.	X		
	Fisher J.H.	X		
	Frost I.W.	X		
	Frost J.T.	X		
Bugler.	Gill T.	X		
	Goldschmidt J.A.	X		

LANDREYS LIGHT HORSE
Also listed as
LANDREYS HORSE Contd.

		Clasps		
		Ba	Tr	Be
Tpr.	Hart T.	X		
	Haupt W.H.	X		
	Herbert Wm.		X	
	Herbert Wm.		X	
	Hewitt C.	X		
	Hughes J.R.		X	
	Jenkins A.E.	X		
	Kelly J.	X	X	
	Kelly W.J.		X	
	Kindness A.	X		
	Koyd J.	X		
	Lawler M.J.	X		
	Luden H.	X		
	Lund J.P.A.	X		
	Marrian F.	X	X	
	Maytham E.W.		X	
	Montleo G.	X		X
	Pereira W.	X		
	Ploetz C.	X		
	Ponton J.A.	X		
	Power E.	X		
	Pyper C.E.			X
	Reynolds J.	X		
	Sanders A.		X	
	Smith A.E.	X	X	
	Smith B.	X		
	Smith J.		X	
	Smith W.	X		
	Smith W.J.		X	
	Spinner A.	X		
	Symons A.		X	
	Symons S.	X		
	Tee J.	X		
	Terry M.	X		
	Thies W.	X		
	Turner A.	X	X	
	Turst E.	X		
	Waberski F.	X		
	Watts C.		X	
	Williams C.		X	
	Williams J.	X		
	Witham T.	X		

LEACHES RIFLES.

		Ba	Tr	Be
Capt.	Westbrook H.	X		X
Lt.	Champneys A.T.	X	X	
	Jones L.M.	X	X	

LEARYS NATIVE LEVIES.

		Ba	Tr	Be
Lt.	Scott D.B.		X	

LERIBE NATIVE LEVY. Also listed as LERIBE LEVY.

		Ba	Tr	Be
Commandant.	Bell C.G.H.	X		X
Lt.	Mc Kay T.	X		
	Shepherd E.R.	X		

LONSDALES RIFLES.

		Ba	Tr	Be
Capt.	Carroll P.J.	X		
	Wood E.G.P.	X		
Lt./Adj.	Carter H.W.	X		

MACLEAR CONSTAB. Also listed as MACLEAR SPL. CONS. MCLEAR NAT. LEVIES

		Ba	Tr	Be
Capt./Adj.	Forbes-Cumming R.		X	
Capt.	Stevenson W.		X	
Lt.	Halliday R.E.	X	X	
	Stevenson J.E.		X	

MAFEKING MOUNTED RIFLES

		Ba	Tr	Be
Cpl.	Cox L.A.			X

MAFETENG CONTINGENT. Also listed as MAFETENG NATIVE CONT. MAFETENG VOLS.

		Ba	Tr	Be
Capt.	Bradshaw A.W.	X		
	Buxton E.W.	X		
	Hancock E.	X		
Lt.	Carlisle W.M.	X		
Pte.	Stevens C.	X		
	Waugh E.	X		

	Clasps		
	Ba	Tr	Be
MALMESBURY BURGHERS.			
Capt. Savoy O.R.D.		X	
Sgt. Ayres R.		X	
Croeser S.F.R.		X	
Sowerby J.A.		X	
Cpl. Relihan H.S.		X	
Tpr./Pte. Bowern A.		X	
Dixon J.E.		X	
Embrose J.		X	
Lochner N.R.	X	X	
Trumpeter.			
Möller E.		X	
Tpr./Pte. Nelson H.D.F.		X	
Peters C.H.		X	
Schenk A.	X		
Schutte J.F.		X	
Smith W.		X	
Wustenhoff J.F.		X	
MALMESBURY LEVIES.			
Lt. Young W.C.	X		
MASERU NATIVE LEVIES.			
Pay & Qms. Broomfield F.O.	X		
MASERU VOLUNTEERS.			
Pte. Collier S.C.	X		
MC NICHOLAS HORSE.			
Sgt. Tyrell L.E.N.		X	
MIDDELBURG BURGHERS.			
Capt. Hughes E.P.	X		
Qms. Stewart J.	X		
Sgt. Trollip J.S.	X		
MOHALI HOEK CONTINGENT Also listed as MAHALES HOEK CONTG.			
Tpr. Mc Carter J.A.	X		

	Clasps		
	Ba	Tr	Be
MOUNT AYLIFF VOL.			
Commandant. Read W.H.		X	
Capt. Blenkinsop W.		X	
MOUNT TEMPLE HORSE.			
Lt. Lanham G.C.			X
Sgt. Day J.W.H.			X
Fitzgerald F.P.			X
Tpr. Claasens J.B.			X
MURRAYSBURG BURGHERS.			
Lt. van Heerden J.L.		X	
MUTERS RANGERS.			
Capt. Muter J. v.d.Byl	X	X	
Sgt. Cutter W.H.	X	X	
Pte. Anderson J.	X	X	
Anderson W.	X	X	
Dengler H.H.	X	X	
Lawrence F.	X	X	
Richardson J.	X	X	
Ross J.	X	X	
Ross J.W.	X	X	
Bugler. Wolff T.E.	X	X	
NATAL CONSTABULARY.			
Lt. Raw W.F.		X	
NATAL MOUNTED POLICE.			
Commandant. Dartnell J.G.	X		
Inspector. Campbell F.A.	X		
Mansel G.	X		
Sub./Insp. Phillips F.L.	X		

NATAL MOUNTED POLICE. contd.

Rank	Name	Ba	Tr	Be
Sgt.	Hobson W.H.	X		
	Masson I.A.	X		
Cpl.	Abraham F.M.	X		
	Chappell C.S.	X		
	Clarke W.J.	X		
	Hamilton C.	X		
	Prendergast A.	X		
L/Cpl.	Knott W.	X		
	Martin C.A.	X		
Tpr.	Campbell W.D.	X		
	Cheesman E.	X		
	Dickinson W.	X		
	Evans F.	X		
	George W.C.H.	X		
	Hall W.	X		
	Harris M. de M.		X	
	Harrod P.	X		
	Mardall G.S.	X		
	Pennefather H.	X		
	Percival C.J.	X		
	Petsch O.	X		
	Pierson J.	X		
	Purcer E.A.	X		
	Tully H.R.	X		
	Vibert C.A.	X		

NATAL MOUNTED RIFLES.

Rank	Name	Ba	Tr	Be
Cpl.	Dorehill W.V.	X		

NATIVE BASUTO LEVY.

Rank	Name	Ba	Tr	Be
Sgt.	Cole F.B.		X	

NATIVE CONTINGENT.

Rank	Name	Ba	Tr	Be
Capt.	Whyte H.B.	X	X	
Lt.	Tonneson T.B.	X		
Sgt.	Atwell J.	X		

NATIVE CONTINGENT TEMBULAND.

Officer Commanding.

Rank	Name	Ba	Tr	Be
	Levey C.J.		X	

NATIVE LEVIES.

Rank	Name	Ba	Tr	Be
Lt.	Webb F.C.	X	X	

NESBITTS LIGHT HORSE.
Also listed as NESBITTS HORSE.

Commandant.

Rank	Name	Ba	Tr	Be
	Nesbitt R.A.	X	X	
Capt.	Cogan J.M.	X	X	
	Hutton A.	X	X	
	Nesbitt R.H.	X		
	Robinson M.B.		X	X
Lt.Qm.	White A.S.	X	X	
Lt.	Bayley H.J.	X	X	
	Brown S.T.	X	X	
	Ham A.	X	X	
	Hannan F.J.H.	X	X	
	Hayton J.E.	X	X	
	Johnson H.C.	X	X	
	Passmore T.W.	X	X	
	Scully W.C.	X	X	
	Walker C.D.	X	X	
Sgt./Maj.	Blue D.	X	X	
	D'Arcy J.H.	X	X	
	Froud A.J.	X	X	
	Hamer G.J.	X	X	
	Lerrick J.	X	X	
	Radcliffe G.	X	X	
Sgt.	Bower J.H.	X	X	
Bugler Sgt.	Brick W.E.	X	X	
Sgt.	Clinton Geo.	X	X	
	Daniel W.H.	X	X	
	Foster A.	X	X	
	Kirby H.W.	X	X	
	Larsen W.J.	X	X	
	Long E.G.	X	X	
	Marshall A.J.	X	X	
	Mc Donald H.	X	X	X
	Maynard H.	X	X	
	Pitt W.J.	X	X	

NESBITTS LIGHT HORSE
Also listed as NESBITTS HORSE. contd.

		Clasps		
		Ba	Tr	Be
Sgt.	Thompsen C.J.	X	X	
	Wasserfall J.	X	X	
Cpl.	Buckley J.	X	X	
	Clementson T.	X	X	
	Gainsford R.	X	X	
	Hohman C.	X	X	
	Newton D.L.	X	X	
Pte./ Tpr.	Allen G.	X	X	
	Allen T.	X		
	Austin D.	X	X	
	Austin W.	X	X	
	Barrable W.T.	X		
	Bilson G.J.	X	X	
	Bishop J.	X		
	Boland T.	X	X	
	Brown A.S.	X	X	
	Brown J.	X	X	
	Burns J.J.	X	X	
	Burgess C.	X	X	
	Campbell J.	X	X	
	Cole G.C.	X	X	
	Cook J.	X	X	
	Curran J.	X	X	X
	Deiring W.	X	X	
	Diggeden F.	X	X	
	Emms W.	X	X	
	Faulds R.H.	X	X	
	Friend R.	X	X	
	Frisch W.	X	X	
	Gaines J.	X	X	
	Goodyer D.	X	X	
	Green E.J.			X
	Groenemeyer A.	X	X	
	Hall C.	X	X	
	Hays A.	X	X	
	Hennings L.	X	X	
	Hoctor M.	X	X	
	Japp G.		X	
Bugler.				
	Jefferson T.	X		
Pte./ Tpr.	Jolly D.	X	X	
	Lawer W^m.	X	X	
	Lawrence W.	X		
	Lowton J.	X	X	
	Lust J.	X	X	X

NESBITTS LIGHT HORSE
Also listed as NESBITTS HORSE contd.

		Clasps		
		Ba	Tr	Be
Bugler.				
	Marsh A.	X	X	
	Marsh S.	X	X	
	Mason S.	X	X	
	Mc Donald D.	X	X	
	Mc Garr A.E.	X	X	
	Merritt F.G.	X	X	
	Nelson M.H.T.	X	X	
	Nielson C.	X	X	X
	O' Brien J.	X	X	
	Page T.	X	X	
	Park C.E.	X	X	
	Parsons C.T.	X	X	
	Philpot F.	X	X	
	Philpot W.	X	X	
	Pryor T.P.		X	
	Quinn W.H.R.	X	X	
	Roberson W.	X	X	
	Ryan M.	X	X	
	Salonika J.	X	X	
	Scheder P.D.	X	X	
	Smith S.C.	X	X	
	Smith W.	X	X	
	Smith W.J.	X	X	
	Strutt S.	X	X	X
	Tendall R.	X	X	
	Thomas A.J.C.	X	X	
	Toughey J.	X	X	
	Trautmann W.H.	X	X	
	Westley A.	X	X	
	Whitaker W.P.	X	X	
	Whitebeard T.E.	X	X	
	Wildey G.	X	X	

ORDNANCE DEPARTMENT.

		Ba	Tr	Be
Lt.Col.	Lanning R.A.			X
Deputy Com.				
	Hamer J.N.	X	X	
	Shiel J.D.		X	
Asst.Comm.				
	Adams R.M.		X	
	Allaway S.A.C.K.	X	X	
	Webster J.A.		X	
Storekeeper.				
	Walsh T.			X

OUDTSHOORN BURGHERS.

Rank	Name	Ba	Tr	Be
Capt.	Ferreira A.H.		X	
	Swemmer J.H.		X	
Lt.	Cummins T.C.B.	X	X	
Sgt./Maj.	Noble F.		X	
Sgt.	Paterson R.B.		X	
	Pienaar J.J.		X	
Cpl.	Brown T.		X	
	Gericke H.S.		X	
	Keyter J.J.		X	
	Rankin T.		X	
Pte./Tpr.	Hardy A.J.		X	
	Hardy J.A.		X	
	Hooper F.R.		X	
	Humbly C.	X	X	
	Mc Mahon T.W.		X	
	O' Grady W.		X	
	Olivier J.S.		X	
	Stokes D.E.		X	
	Wolmarans G.F.E.		X	

OUDTSHOORN VOLUNTEER RIFLES.

Rank	Name	Ba	Tr	Be
Lt.	Bawden J.			X
Coy S.M.	Bain J.			X
Sgt.Ins.	Murray J.			X
Sgt.	Sullivan J.			X
Cpl.	Nel C.P.			X
	Vos W.			X
	Wallis W.J.			X
L/Cpl.	Elliott F.W.		X	
	Helfritz P.			X
	Puren J.M.			X
Pte.	Aspelling H.			X
	Borcherds N.B.			X
	Cowley J.G.			X
	Cook C.			X
	Falconer W.			X

OUDTSHOORN VOLUNTEER RIFLES Contd.

Rank	Name	Ba	Tr	Be
Pte.	Fivaz A.			X
	Froode H.			X
	Giles J.T.			X
	Gilliespie E.A.			X
	Groll A.			X
	Harris J.B.			X
	Heaney J.			X
	Joynt H.P.J.S.			X
	Keyter G.T.			X
	King G.			X
	Meyer A.L.			X
	Meyer N.W.			X
	Meeser N.			X
	Moore L.W.			X
	Roslee F.			X
	Scott D.C.			X
	Scott H.R.			X
	Scott J.			X
	Scott W.J.			X
	Silk M.			X
	Tesnar J.			X
	Thorpe F.G.			X
	Thorpe J.			X
	v.d. Westhuizen A.			X
	Vos C.			X
	Wyness R.F.G.			X
	Zinn A.W.			X

<u>Note:</u> L/CPL. ELLIOTT- CLASPS TRANSKEI.

According to the Regimental returns L/Cpl. Elliott served in Bechuanaland. The Oudtshoorn Volunteer Rifles were formed in 1890 and could not have seen action in the Transkei.
The Medal Roll also shows a Private F.W. Elliott as having received the Medal with Clasp Bechuanaland.

PAARL BURGHERS.

Rank	Name	Ba	Tr	Be
Lt.Adj.	le Roux G.H.	X	X	
Lt.	Coaton A.B.	X	X	
Sgt./Maj.	Pentz P.J.	X	X	
Sgt.	Blake T.J.	X		
	Curlewis J.F.I.	X	X	
Cpl.	Snow A.	X	X	
Pte./Tpr.	Baldwin W.P.	X	X	
	Bauer L.	X	X	
	Busby T.	X	X	
	Christoffels S.C.	X		
	Conning T.	X		
	English F.	X	X	
	Frick C.C.		X	
	Irving W.	X	X	
	Kelly J.F.		X	
	Lurssen L.C.		X	
	Marais J.F.	X	X	
	Marchand B.		X	
	Mc Court J.H.	X		
	Rossouw J.M.	X	X	
	Thompson P.		X	
	Trusler H.	X	X	
	Vos H.C.	X		
	Wernberg W.A.O.		X	

PAARL WESTERN LEVIES.

Rank	Name	Ba	Tr	Be
Pte.	Almeida E.	X	X	

PAPKUIL RIFLES. Also listed as PAPKUIL MOUNTED RIFLE CLUB.

Rank	Name	Ba	Tr	Be
Capt.	Pringle W.S.L.		X	
Lt.	Pringle J.St. L.S.		X	
S/Maj.	Todd J.M.		X	
Sgt.	Hibbert J.		X	
	Middleton H.M.		X	

PAPKUIL RIFLES. Also listed as PAPKUIL MOUNTED RIFLE CLUB. Contd.

Rank	Name	Ba	Tr	Be
Cpl.	Daly S.K.C.	?	?	?
	van der Merwe A.			X
	Venter A.P.			X
Tpr.	Grissel H.J.			X
	Grissel J.J.			X
	Havenga H.S.			X
	van der Merwe J.J.H.			X
	Voss C.A.			X

PORT ELIZABETH RIFLES.

Rank	Name	Ba	Tr	Be
Lt.	Russell J.B.	X		
Pte.	Lamont H.H.	X		

PRINCE ALBERT BURGHERS.

Rank	Name	Ba	Tr	Be
Qms.	Wilson W.K.		X	
Sgt.	Serrurier J.		X	

PRINCE ALFREDS OWN CAPE VOL.ARTILLERY. Also listed as P.A.O.C.A.

Rank	Name	Ba	Tr	Be
Maj.	Inglesby T.J.			X
Surgeon.	Smartt T.W.		X	
Lt.	Anderson K.			X
Lt./Adj.	Duff B.M.		X	
Lt.	Mc Lachlan W.		X	
S/M.	Williams G.N.			X
Conductor.	Boon J.J.		X	
B.S.M.	Stanford W.		X	
Qms.	Bayly B.		X	
	Reid G.A.			X
	Thomas W.E.			X
Bqms.	Bates G.F.		X	
Sgt./Trump.	Taylor C.R.			X

PRINCE ALFREDS OWN CAPE VOL. ARTILLERY Also listed as P.A.O.C.A. contd.

Rank	Name	Ba	Tr	Be
Sgt.	Flack E.J.		X	
	Fletcher W.B.			X
	Graham A.B.		X	
	Hazell T.H.		X	
	Short G.		X	
	Smith S.J.			X
	Woodhead L.		X	
	Yallop E.			X
Cpl.	Amyot W.T.		X	
	Arnold W.			X
	Cooper J.W.		X	
	Rennie A.L.		X	
	Stumke J.C.A.			X
Bomb.	Cannon E.L.			X
	Divine F.W.		X	
	Eckard C.S.		X	
	Grant J.		X	
	Moyle C.M.			X
	Price E.J.			X
	Reid H.A.		X	
	Rose A.W.J.			X
Gunner.	Abbot W.D.A.		X	
	Backwall S.T.			X
	Barnes F.E.			X
	Bennett H.J.			X
Driver.	Bobbins J.	X	X	X
Gunner.	Brown S.			X
	Crosby H.P.			X
Driver.	Davison C.R.		X	
Gunner.	Dodwell E.P.V.		X	
	Doherty H.H.			X
Shoeing Smith.	Douglass C.J.B.			X
Gunner.	Faulkner T.J.		X	X
	Freeman G.H.		X	
	Graves J.A.		X	
	Grey H.G.			X
	Hairbottle J.W.			X
	Hancock R.R.			X
	Heckroodt J de V.		X	
	Hughes C.		X	

PRINCE ALFREDS OWN CAPE VOL. ARTILLERY also listed as P.A.O.C.A. contd.

Rank	Name	Ba	Tr	Be
Gunner.	Jardine G.		X	
	Johnson H.J.			X
	Jones W.J.			X
	Laing W.		X	
	Lawton J.D.		X	
	Linley A.E.			X
	Miller A.R.			X
	Ramsden H.E.			X
Trumpeter.	Rees A.		X	X
Driver.	Reid B.B.		X	
Gunner.	Revington J.D.			X
	Ricketts E.W.			X
	Schonegevel O.C.		X	
	Shelroke G.E.			X
Driver.	Thallon J.			X
	Tomlinson A.M.			X
Gunner.	Ulrich W.E.		X	
	v.d. Schyff M.H.		X	
	Vos D.J.R.		X	
	Vos P.		X	
	Woodhead M.		X	
	Woods W.			X
	Weankmore J.T.		X	
	Wright F.			X

PRINCE ALFREDS VOLUNTEER GUARD.

Rank	Name	Ba	Tr	Be
Maj.	Deare G.R.	X		
Chaplain.	Wirgman A.T.	X		
Capt.	Court H.W.			X
	Little A.	X		
	Mc Andrew J.R.			X
	Murrell G.			X
Lt./Adj.	Purland T.T.C.	X		

PRINCE ALFREDS VOLUNTEER GUARDS. Contd.

Rank	Name	Ba	Tr	Be
Lt.	Back W.G.	X		
	Elliott C.G.	X		
	Leeds F.W.			X
	Tudhope F.S.	X		
	Wares A.P.J.			X
Sub/Lt.	Thornton J.M.	X		
Sgt./Maj.	Geary T.	X		
	White J.	X		
Bugle Major Sgt.				
	Braybrooke J.			X
Qms.	Beadle A.			X
Col. Sgt.	Payne J.W.			X
	Stock J.W.	X		
Arm./Sgt.	Kemsley P.			X
Staff Sgt.				
	Everitt A.P.	X		
Pay/Sgt.	Clarry R.W.	X		
	Scholefield F.H.	X		
Sgt.	Archibald W.R.			X
	Bain N.M.	X		
	Banwell E.J.	X		
	Bashford H.F.			X
	Braybrooke J.			X
	Brooks W.H.			X
	Dix-Peek St. G.			X
	Emslie R.			X
	Ferguson A.W.	X		
	Geerdts W.H.	X		
	Leschinsky R.			X
	Mc Kay L.	X		
	Pattison F.V.			X
	Perry C.E.			X
	Phelan E.J.	X	X	
	Stumke C.F.	X		
	Trader J.T.	X		
	Thompson R.P.	X		
	Walker W.C.			X
Cpl.Bugler.				
	Wiley T.	X		

PRINCE ALFREDS VOLUNTEER GUARDS. Contd.

Rank	Name	Ba	Tr	Be
Cpl.	Aitkin J.	X		
	Bodile G.	X		
	Damerall W.E.			X
	Dyke E.S.C.	X		X
	Green F.			X
	Henderson J.	X		
	Innes W.			X
	Johnson A.C.	X		
	Little A.	X		
	Long J.L.			X
	Mitchley P.	X		
	Murray J.	X		
	Murray M.	X		
	North V.H.			X
	Rennie A.L.		X	
	Robertson E.P.			X
	Rundle T.J.	X		
L/Cpl.	Armstrong E.H.B.			X
	Beere A.H.			X
	Cardno A.G.	X		X
	Holland G.L.S.	X		X
	Hunt W.H.			X
	Johnson R.D.	X		X
	Morgan E.V.			X
	O'Grady B.H.	X		
	O'Hara F.G.	X	X	
	Reid J.L.			X
	Rice H.H.W.			X
	Snow B.J.			X
	Southey G.L.	X		X
	Whitney W.P.			X
Bugler.				
	Harding P.W.			X
	Lauder J.H.			X
Pte.	Ablett R.J.G.	X		
	Armstrong W.R.	X		
	Arter H.C.			X
	Artz M.	X		
	Artz P.	X		X
	Auret J.B.	X		X
	Bayley H.	X		
	Baker W.			X
	Barns S.H.			X
	Bassett T.			X
	Bates F.C.	X		X
	Batt W.H.			X
	Beck J.G.	X		
	Beck G.			X
	Beckett J.C.	X		

PRINCE ALFREDS VOLUNTEER GUARD. Contd.

Rank	Name	Ba	Tr	Be
Pte.	Beckford J.	X		
	Berry C.	X		
	Berry J.L.	X		
	Berry W.	X		
	Blackburn G.A.			X
	Boyd W.J.	X	X	
	Braithwaite S.			X
	Brophy T.	X		
	Brown J.	X	X	
	Buchanan W.	X		
	Cameron A.E.	X		
	Campbell W.Mc L.			X
	Carroll J.	X		X
	Carter F.			X
	Castleman A.			X
	Chinnery G.H.	X		
	Clarke J.A.			X
	Clewlow W.	X		X
	Cogill A.	X		
	Cole R.			X
	Coleman G.			X
	Cook B.R.			X
	Cooke W.H.			X
	Cooke J.W.			X
	Copeland G.C.			X
	Coppard W.John	X		
	Corbett C.			X
	Corbett F.W.			X
	Cunningham J.A.	X		
	Darlow G.	X		
	Davis B.			X
	Dienelt R.			X
	Dignon J.	X		
	Dix Peek D.			X
	Don A.L.			X
	Don D.G.	X		
	Dorrington H.J.W.	X		
	Downing T.A.B.			X
	Dowse F.W.	X		
	Duffy W.B.	X		X
	Durban C.	X		
	Dury E.R.	X		
	Edwards R.H.D.			X
	Ellis T.	X		
	Fairlamb H.			X
	Feather J.J.	X		
	Fenix T.H.			X
	Finch W.H.			X
	Fitzgerald E.M.	X		
	Fitzgerald G.J.	X		
	Fleming W.			X

PRINCE ALFREDS VOLUNTEER GUARD. Contd.

Rank	Name	Ba	Tr	Be
Pte.	Ford A.J.			X
	Fowler W.	X		
	Fraser J.	X		
	Frost J.P.	X		
	Furniss H.			X
	Gamble F.F.	X		
Bandsman.	Galer E.	X		
Pte.	Gardiner E.H.			X
	Geerdts W.H.	X		
	Gibbs J.A.	X		
	Grasstorff W.	X		
	Grigg W.H.			X
	Harris E.J.			X
	Hearn A.K.			X
	Hearne E.J.P.			X
	Henderson W.F.			X
	Heybyrne W.E.			X
	Hoey J.	X		
	Hogan T.			X
	Holton F.G.	X		
	Hooper J.	X		
	Howitz L.W.F.			X
	Hunt F.			X
	Jackson G.	X		
	Jackson T.	X		
	Jarvis W.E.	X		
	Jenkins A.H.	X		
	John W.			X
	Jones E.	X		
	Jordon J.			X
	Keats R.			X
	Kemmy B.			X
	Kenny P.J.			X
	Kenny T.	X		
	Kydd J.	X		
	Leahy T.P.	X		
	Leary J.	X		
	Le Vershea L.L.			X
	Lohrentz W.J.F.	X		
	Longden W.M.	X		
	Makins J.G.	X		
	Mandy E.			X
	Marran C.H.	X		
	Mason W.J.			X
	Matthews A.B.	X		
	Matthews S.	X		
	Mc Kenzie G.C.			X
	Mc Kenzie R.			X
	Mc Leod J.	X		

PRINCE ALFREDS VOLUNTEER GUARDS. Contd.

		Ba	Tr	Be
Pte.	Mc Loughlin A.	X		
	Mc Namara J.	X		
	Mc Nair J.			X
	Mc Williams J.			X
	Menier J.A.	X		
	Milne J.			X
	Mitchley J.S.	X		
	Murphy M.			X
	Murray C.	X		
	Negus E.P.			X
	Neville A.E.			X
	Nevin R.H.	X		
	Noble R.A.			X
	Nothard W.	X		
	Nystrom A.			X
	O'Brien J.	X		
	Oram F.H.C.			X
	Osche R.			X
	Owen T.J.			X
	Parker T.W.			X
	Partridge H.			X
	Passmore W.H.M.	X		
	Peacock W.J.			X
	Perry W.	X		
	Petersen H.W.			X
	Philpot W.	X		
	Pirie J.R.	X		
	Pirie W.	X		
	Pringle E.	X		
	Ratchford J.			X
	Reeve T.			X
	Reeve W.			X
	Reid R.			X
	Rigg H.C.J.			X
	Roberts D.			X
	Roberts Fred	X		
	Robertson D.	X		
	Rosher C.H.	X		
	Rudd Alex	X		
	Rutherford A.			X
	Schultz J.B.			X
	Short A.J.	X		
	Simpson A.			X
	Smith A. Mc B.			X
	Smith J.	X		
	Smith W.A.			X
	Stanley G.	X		
	Steers W.W.	X		
	Sterley G.J.	X		
	Stewart H.C.			X

PRINCE ALFREDS VOLUNTEER GUARDS. Contd.

		Ba	Tr	Be
Pte.	Stuart W.	X		
	Stockholm C.			X
	Swann M.A.	X		
	Swanson H.A.	X		
	Swanson J.	X		
	Sweeting J.T.			X
	Syer J.			X
	Tatchet P.J.			X
	Taylor H.A.			X
	Taylor J.			X
	Thomas F.R.			X
	Thomas T.	X		
	Thomson R.P.	X		
	Thorne W.	X		
	Tonks H.E.	X		
	Townsend T.	X		
	Tracey W.A.	X		
	Wall W.	X		
	Walton G.A.			X
	Watson C.H.	X		
	Werthiemer A.	X		
	Wheeler W.			X
	Willcocks A.H.			X
	White R.	X		
	Whiteley J.E.	X		
	Whyte R.W.			X
	Whyte W.			X
	Wilkerson A.T.			X
	Williams I.			X
	Williamson G.			X

PULLENS HORSE.

		Ba	Tr	Be
Tpr.	Townshend H.Mc K.		X	

PULLENS RANGERS.

		Ba	Tr	Be
Cpl.	Turner W.	X		

QUEENSTOWN BURGHERS.
Also listed as QUEENSTOWN Vol.

		Ba	Tr	Be
Capt.	Stubbs W.R.	X		
Qms.	Wyatt B.	X	X	
Sgt.	Moore F.W.G.	X	X	
	Pote M.P.	X	X	

QUEENSTOWN BURGHERS.
Also listed as
QUEENSTOWN VOL. Contd.

		Clasps		
		Ba	Tr	Be
Cpl.	Mc Kenzie A.	X	X	
	Watson W.G.	X		
Bugler.				
	Mc Kay D.	X		
Tpr./	Barends G.	X		
Pte.	Bousfield H.R.	X		
	Cockson W.		X	
	Hoskin H.S.	X	X	
	Kelly J.	X		
	Ludwig F.W.	X	X	
	Maytham A.C.	X	X	
	Rex J.O.	X	X	
	Thorn J.P.	X		
	Trembling J.	X		
	van Wyn Gaarden J.P.	X		

QUEENSTOWN DIVISION.

		Ba	Tr	Be
Tpr.	Driscoll T.		X	

QUEENSTOWN FLYING COL.

		Ba	Tr	Be
Lt.	Cooper W.		X	

QUEENSTOWN RIFLE VOLUNTEERS.

		Ba	Tr	Be
Capt.	Berry W.A.			X
Lt.	Humphreys H.H.			X
Rsm.	Baker W.A.			X
Csm.	Couper R.			X
	Lloyd C.W.			X
Band Sgt.				
	Andrews E.			X
Sgt.	Holl G.			X
	Houlgate F.J.			X
	Jamieson J.H.			X
Cpl.	Butow A.G.			X
	Paetzold A.			X
	Popjoy W.			X

QUEENSTOWN RIFLE VOLUNTEER Contd.
L/

		Clasps		
		Ba	Tr	Be
Cpl.	Austen E.H.			X
	Cook J.			X
	Doyle W.K.			X
	Edwards C.			X
	Scandrett A.B.			X
	Stead G.F.			X
Pte.	Barnes C.R.			X
	Blake W.J.		X	
	Bradshaw A.			X
	Bushell W.G.			X
	Clack W.H.C.			X
	Crumplin E.J.			X
	Crumplin W.H.			X
	Davie S.T.			X
	Davison J.			X
	de Stadler L.A.			X
	Fenter M.A.			X
	Foley J.M.			X
	Francis R.	X		X
	Frazer A.			X
	Goldman W.B.			X
	Hart F.J.			X
	Hartley W.B.			X
	Holl A.			X
	Hooper C.			X
	Jeffrey E.W.H.			X
	Jones H.M.			X
	Jordaan J.W.			X
	Lambole J.			X
	Langfield H.E.			X
	Liefeldt B.C.			X
	Liefeldt T.E.			X
	Mardon R.J.			X
	Marshall R.H.			X
	Mathews A.E.			X
	Maybury H.J.C.			X
	Mc Gee T.L.			X
	Palmer P.G.			X
	Parry T.E.			X
	Patrick H.H.			X
	Preston W.T.		X	
	Richards J.B.			X
	Robinson J.I.			X
	Roden F.G.			X
	Seaton T.			X
	Sinclair R.			X
	Smale F.W.			X
	Smith A.E.			X
	Smith A.G.			X

Unit / Rank / Name	Ba	Tr	Be
QUEENSTOWN RIFLE VOLUNTEERS. contd.			
Pte. Strong F.W.			X
Styles J.			X
Thomson W.			X
Venter H.			X
Von Broembsen G.A.			X
Von Sychowski E.F.			X
Webster A.R.			X
QUMBU CONTINGENT.			
Officer Commanding.			
Mc Glashan P.		X	
QUTHENG & MASITISI NATIVE CONTG. Also listed as NATIVE POLICE QUITHING CONTG.			
Sub.Insp. Humphreys A.R.	X		
RICHMOND BURGHERS.			
Capt. Dyason A.	X		
Qms. Pavitt R.A.C.	X		
Sgt. Albert R. (Should be R.A.C.Pavitt)	X		
Cpl. Nicholson C.S.	X		
Pte. Brider E.	X		
Pavard J.	X		
Tpr. Somers J.	X		
Spiethoff E.	X		
Pte. van Heerden D.J.	X		
ROSS AND HICKSONS HORSE.			
Capt. Hickson-Mahony J.C.	X	X	

Unit / Rank / Name	Ba	Tr	Be
ROSS LIGHT HORSE Also listed as ROSS HORSE.			
Capt. Ross C.J.		X	
Lt. Beer F.		X	
Cpl. Jacobs J.		X	
Skinner J.	X	X	
Tpr./Pte. Hagan E.H.		X	X
Harvett J.W.		X	
Kindness G.		X	
Lagaese F.		X	
Miller W.		X	
Otten C.H.		X	
Parsons T.		X	X
Rundell J.M.		X	
ROYAL IRISH FUSILEERS (3RD) Also listed as 3RD ROYAL 1 RIFLES.			
Capt. Girdwood R.H.			X
SALEM RANGERS.			
Tpr. Querl A.	X		
SCHERMANS BURGHERS.			
Sp.Const. Aucamp			X
SCOUTS.			
Lt. Bowman F.M.		X	
SEVENTH HUSSARS. Also listed as 7th HUSSARS.			
Lt. Wormald C.F.W.			X
Pte. Cope G.			X
SIXTHIETH RIFLES 3RD. Listed also as 3rd 60th RIFLES.			
Maj. Terry A.F.		X	
Lt. Mc Grigor C.R.R.		X	

	Clasps		
	Ba	Tr	Be

SIXTIETH RIFLES - 3RD
Listed also as 3RD 60th RIFLES Contd.

Rank	Name	Ba	Tr	Be
Col./Sgt.	Ovenston E.F.		X	
Bugler.	Such A.	X		
Pte.	Sheldrake E.		X	

SOMERSET EAST BURGHERS
Also listed as SOMERSET EAST CONT.

Rank	Name	Ba	Tr	Be
Lt.	Pavey E.J.	X		
Sgt./Maj.	Hannan E.C.W.	X		
Sgt.	Holiday F.	X		
Cpl.	Berry J.F.	X		
Pte.	Attesbury W.G.	X		
Tpr.	Bateman J.	X		
	Boyce G.	X		
	Coulon W.	X		
Pte.	Cross H.	X		
	Cross J.	X		
	Denny F.E.	X		
Tpr.	De Beer J.	X		
	Erasmus J.A.	X		
Pte.	Fisher F.	X		
Tpr.	Klein L.	X		
Pte.	Rosendorff M.	X		
Tpr.	Rundle H.	X		
	Smith W.H.	X		

SOUTHEYVILLE LEVIES.

Rank	Name	Ba	Tr	Be
Capt.	Fenix G.		X	

SPECIAL BORDER POLICE

Rank	Name	Ba	Tr	Be
Capt.	Brislin A.C.	X	X	
Tpr.	Harris G.E.	X	X	

STANFORDS POLICE.
Also listed as STANFORDS SPECIAL POLICE.

Rank	Name	Ba	Tr	Be
Lt.	Chaband C.W.		X	
Pte.	Fitzgerald T.	X	X	

STANTONS LIGHT HORSE.
Also listed as STANTONS HORSE.

Rank	Name	Ba	Tr	Be
Qms.	Leonard P.J.	X		
Sgt.	Moffatt W.	X		
Cpl.	Delaney M.	X		
	Murray F.E.	X		
	O'Grady P.	X		
Tpr.	Davies G.H.	X		
	Hensher W.J.	X		
	Kelly J.	X		
	Ward J.M.	X		

STELLALAND LIGHT HORSE
Also listed as STELLALAND HORSE.

Rank	Name	Ba	Tr	Be
Capt.	Dennison C.G.			X
Surgeon.	Hancock J.E.			X
Lt.	Cullinan A.			X
Sgt./Maj.	Comley C.P.			X
	Seaward H.W.			X
Sgt.	Trollope W.W.			X
Pte.	Bates F.S.			X
	de Beer M.J.			X
	Engelbrecht J.P.G.			X
	Hodgman W.T.			X
	Parsons J.M.J.J.			X
	Pieterse P.A.			X
	Poulton W.J.C.			X
	Purchase B.			X
	Sadler W.G.			X
	Sargeant S.S.			X
	Trollope G.H.			X
	Trollope G.V.			X

STELLENBOSCH BURGHERS.

Commandant.

Rank	Name	Ba	Tr	Be
	Uys J.D.J.		X	
Lt.	Van Kerken G.		X	
Cpl.	Louw J.P. de V.		X	
Tpr./Pte.	Blatherwick T.		X	
	Cannon F.W.		X	
	Cruywagen J.G.	X	X	
	Firmin M.L.	X	X	
	Haupt P.W.		X	
	Jones C.C.	X	X	

Bugler.

Rank	Name	Ba	Tr	Be
	Liesching G.		X	
Tpr./Pte.	Rennick J.		X	
	Wilcock O.	X	X	

STERKSTROOM RIFLES.

Rank	Name	Ba	Tr	Be
Capt.	Sidwell A.	X		

STOCKENSTROOM BURGHERS
Also listed as
STOCKENSTROOM VOLS.
STOCKENSTROOM VOL.RIFLES.

Rank	Name	Ba	Tr	Be
Qms.	Green G.H.	X		
Pte.	Brown J.N.	X		
	Smit J.F.	X		

STOCKENSTROOM HOTT. CONTG.
Also listed as
STOCKENSTROOM CONTG.
STOCKENSTROOM LEVIES.

Rank	Name	Ba	Tr	Be
Lt.	Bunn H.H.		X	
S/Lt.	Kleinbooi K.		X	
Cpl.	Smit J.F.		X	
Tpr.	Meyer J.	X		

STOCKENSTROOM RANGERS.

Rank	Name	Ba	Tr	Be
Sgt./Maj.	Cutter T.G.	X	X	
Tpr.	Campfield H.	X	X	
	Muller C.E.	X	X	

STRACHANS NATIVE CONTG.
Also listed as
STRACHANS NAT. LEVIES.

Rank	Name	Ba	Tr	Be
Capt./Paym.	Erskine St. V.W.		X	
Lt.	Mc Gregor F.	X	X	

STUTTERHEIM L. 1 VOLS.
Also listed as
STUTTERHEIM VOLS.

Rank	Name	Ba	Tr	Be
Col./Sgt.	Ewers V.	?	?	?
Cpl.	Grunewald T.O.	X		
	Rudolph H.	X		
Pte.	Hansel F.	X		
	Keifer W.	X		
	Schwulst A.	X		
	Steinhofel G.	X		

SWELLENDAM BURGHERS.

Rank	Name	Ba	Tr	Be
Lt.	Van Eeden A.H.		X	
Qms.	Marcus H.C.		X	
Cpl.	Dixon J.		X	
	Mc Gregor W.C.		X	
Pte./Tpr.	Beyers C.F.		X	
	Bosman A.		X	
	Diederechs C.H.		X	
	Du Toit ??		X	
	Fullard W.		X	
	Linde P.E.S.		X	
	Rademan D.C.		X	
	Rademan H.J.L.		X	
	Siebert H.B.	X		
	Solms G.		X	

TAMBOOKIE WARD BURGHERS.

Rank	Name	Ba	Tr	Be
Capt.	Kelly J.J.	X		

TARKASTAD BURGHERS.
Also listed as TARKA B.

Rank	Name	Ba	Tr	Be
Capt.	Erasmus D.J.		X	
Cpl.	Temlett J.R.	X	X	

Unit / Name	Ba	Tr	Be
TARKASTAD BURGHERS. Also listed as **TARKA B.** contd.			
Pte./Tpr. Coetzer D.P.		X	
Hattingh G.M.		X	
Hogan W.	X		
Hürter C.J.M.		X	X
Stow G.		X	
Stow J.		X	
Tannahill J.	X		
Wright E.C.	X	X	
TARKA VOLUNTEER RIFLES.			
Capt. Dowdle P.H.		X	
Lt. Patrick A.		X	
TAUNGS GUN DETACHMENT.			
Sgt./Ins. Morris A.F.M.			X
TELEGRAPHIC & INTELLIGENCE STAFF.			
No Rank. Forbes J.M.			X
TEMBU LEVIES. Also listed as **TEMBULAND F.F.**			
Capt. Calverley R.W.		X	
Leary J.G.		X	
Capt. Paym. Tainton L.G.H.		X	
Lt. Money G.	X	X	
THOMPSON RELIEF COLUMN			
Capt. Hilliard C.H.		X	X
TRANS M.R.			
Surgeon. Lt. Smyth-Temple			X

Unit / Name	Ba	Tr	Be
TRANSKEI NATIVE CONTINGENT Also listed as **TRANSKEI NATIVE MILITIA. TRANSKEI NATIVE LEVIES. TRANSKEI FINGO MILITIA**			
Commandant. Henley S. St.J.			X
Capt. Clarke W.J.		X	
Girdwood J.G.		X	
Godfrey W.P.		X	
Thompson N.O.		X	
Thornton G.E.		X	X
Lt. Hamilton J.		X	
Holmes L.			X
Johnson F.C.			X
Phillips B.J.		X	
Turnbull G.K.			X
Sgt. Hadley W.			X
Harty G.D.			X
TRANSPORT CORPS.			
Capt. Da Fonseca S.T.			X
Lt. Macbeth J.			X
Ass.Tp. & Com. Off. Welstead A.B.			X
Ass. Tp. Off. Smith A.J.			X
Conductor. Chappe P.L.	X	X	
Doyle E.J.			X
Fischer C.V.	X		
Mortimer M.J.			X
Siebel H.L.	X	X	
Sgt./Maj. Hancocks F.E.			X
Sgt. Poulton F.J.			X
Driver. Fraser C.		X	

		Clasps		
		Ba	Tr	Be

TRANSPORT CORPS.

		Ba	Tr	Be
Tpr.	Fredman W.			X
	Kindness J.			X
	Longmore C.C.			X
	Symons F.			X
	Wahl L.W.			X
Pte.	Gordon F.			X
	Gray A.			X
	Meintjes P.F.			X
	Tanner A.			X
	Tarpley W.			X
	Uren J.			X

TRANSVAAL HORSE.

Colonel.

		Ba	Tr	Be
	Ferreira I.P.	X		
Capt.	Barratt D.A.	X		
	Sinclair J.W.		X	
Lt./Paym.	Immink J.C.	X		
Lt.	Finch E.W.	X		
	Maclean A.B.	X		
	Preston A.P.	X		
	Rathbone C.R.	X		
	Warrington G.	X		
Sgt./Maj.	Berry M.	X		
Sgt.	Cadle J.	X		
	Cawood J.E.	X		
	Keeley D.	X		
	Pakenham C.W.	X		
Cpl.	Conley M.	X		
	Prinslow H.	X	X	
	Schutte S.R.	X		
Pte./Tpr.	Abraham W.J.	X		
	Barns G.D.	X		
	Bobbington W.	X		
	Burnes T.H.	X		
	Carew P.	X		
	Carr H.	X		
	Chapman J.R.	X		
	Conroy T.	X		

TRANSVAAL HORSE Contd.

		Ba	Tr	Be
Pte./	Daniells W.		X	
Tpr.	Dowe J.J.	X		
	Durand W.C.	X		
	Easton A.J.	X		
	Gallagher W.	X		
	Johnson H.	X		
	Johnson W.	X		
	Mc Mullen J.	X		
	Orman H.	X		
	Parsons A.J.	X		
	Pattinson M.	X	X	
	Pearson G.A.	X		

(Note in Medal Roll says not granted the Medal - Rebel.)

		Ba	Tr	Be
	Plumb R.	X		
	Quinn T.	X	X	
	Rosslee J.M.	X		
	Santauna R.	X		
	Scott W.J.	X		
	Sharpe D.	X		
	Van Dyk J.	X		
	White F.	X		

TRUE BLUES.

		Ba	Tr	Be
Tpr.	Taylor S.		X	

TSOLO NAT MILITIA.
Also listed as TSOLO NAT LEVIES. TSOLO NAT CONT.

		Ba	Tr	Be
Lt.	Berry E.J.		X	
	Hudson E.W.		X	
Pte.	Klaas P.		X	

UITENHAGE BURGHERS.

		Ba	Tr	Be
Capt.	Kirkman W.N.		X	
Cpl.	Ashburner R.J.		X	
	de Lange M.C.	X	X	
	du Preez S.J.		X	
	Turner W.	X	X	
Pte./Tpr.	Bonthuys B.C.		X	
	De Meilleon G.		X	
	Harrod W.		X	

UITENHAGE BURGHERS. Contd.

		Ba	Tr	Be
Pte./Tpr.	Lloyd J.P.	X	X	
	Rossam G.		X	
	Van Antwerpen M.J.		X	
	Walker H.		X	
	Welgemoed A.J.	X	X	

UMTATA VOLUNTEERS. Also listed as UMTATA MOUNTED VOLUNTEERS. UMTATA NATIVE CONTINGENT.

		Ba	Tr	Be
Commandant.				
	Stanford A.H.B.		X	
Capt.	Cowie R.J.		X	
	Heathcote J.R.		X	
	Sweeney C.J.		X	
Lt.	Cavanagh W.		X	
S/Maj.	Sell J.H.		X	
Qms.	Spalding J.J.		X	
Sgt.	Black D.		X	
	Hampson W.		X	
Pte.	Brunette S.R.		X	
	Davis D.		X	
	Domoney J.	X	X	
	Goss J.W.R.	X	X	
	Lewis G.R.M.		X	
	O'Leary B.		X	
	Phillipson R.M.		X	
	Shepstone W.		X	
	Turnbull D.H.			X

UPINGTON SPECIAL POLICE.

		Ba	Tr	Be
Pte.	Visser G.		X	

USHERS CONTINGENT.

		Ba	Tr	Be
Pte.	Turner A.	X	X	X

USHERS RANGERS.

		Ba	Tr	Be
Cpl.	Watson J.R.		X	
Pte.	Goatley E.O.		X	
Tpr.	Usher A.	X		

VICTORIA RANGERS. Also listed as VICTORIAN RANGERS. VIC RNGS M^{td} POLICE. VICTORIA WEST RANGERS.

		Ba	Tr	Be
Lt.	Greaves J.W.		X	
Sgt.	Kennedy W.		X	
	Warren F.J.		X	
Cpl.	Murphy H.		X	
	Sullivan T.		X	
Pte.	Buchan J.			X
	Eckhardt N.J.		X	
Bugler.				
	Eyre E.		X	
Pte.	Gabriel A.		X	
	Gabriel J.		X	
	Lennox P.W.		X	
	Malongven A.	X	X	
	Mangan J.		X	
	Morrison N.		X	
	Shannon F.J.		X	
	Shipman A.		X	
	Weber A.		X	
	Williams T.		X	

VICTORIA RIFLES.

		Ba	Tr	Be
Pte.	Sadler W.C.			X

VOLUNTEER MEDICAL STAFF CORPS. Also listed as V.M.S.C. V. MEDICAL STAFF CORPS.

		Ba	Tr	Be
Surgeon Major.				
	Cox J.H.			X
Surgeon.				
	Bensusan A.			X
Cpl.	Gott A.H.		X	
	Whibley P.			X
L/Cpl.	Miller C.A.			X
Pte.	Breeds W.			X
	Gorton T.C.			X
	Hamilton S.M.			X
	Herley H.F.E.			X
	Hickman G.			X
	Hunt S.G.			X
	Rigby W.			X

VRYBURG VOLUNTEERS. Also listed as VRYBURG BURGHERS. VRYBURG MOUNTED VOLUNTEERS.

		Ba	Tr	Be
Capt./Adj.	O'Donoghue J.			X
Capt.	Beaumont A.			X
	Young J.			X
Lt.	Arnot J.R.O.			X
	Brooks H.H.			X
Rsm.	Fraser H.			X
S/M.	Fraser J.C.			X
	Stevens G.H.			X
	Townshend P.			X
Farr. Sgt.	Smith T.			X
Sgt.	Tillard L.O.			X
	van Niekerk P.C.			X
Cpl.	Attwell H.P.			X
	Dalziel J.M.			X
Tpr./Pte.	Atwell K.C.L.			X
	de Klerk W.A.J.			X
	Dunbar W.J.			X
	Edwards E.A.			X
	Fromme G.B.			X
	Halkett W.			X
	Harvey A.R.			X
	Harvey G.M.			X
	Hilton A.			X
	Hilton J.			X
	Hons C.			X
	Hughes R.S.			X
	Ibbetson A.M.W.			X
	Mc Farlane A.			X
	Mc Farlane D.			X
	Mc Loone C.			X
	Moroney P.W.			X
	Sargent S.S.			X
	Simpson C.E.			X
	Tiffin J.			X
	Train B.R.			X
	van Rensburg J.J.			X
	van Rensburg T.J.J.			X

VRYBURG VOLUNTEERS. Also listed as VRYBURG BURGHERS VRYBURG MOUNTED VOLUNTEERS contd.

		Ba	Tr	Be
Pte./Tpr.	Young A.H.			X
Spec. Police.	Visagie A.			X

WALKERS RIFLES.

		Ba	Tr	Be
Lt.	Stirling W.	X	X	
Sgt./Maj.	Burns M.	X	X	
	Dunn J.	X	X	
Sgt.	Austin H.A.	X	X	
Cpl.	Line W.	X	X	
	Sleigh H.R.	X	X	
Pte.	Brown A.E.	X	X	
	Crichton J.	X	X	
	Holmes G.F.	X	X	
	Hunt W.E.	X	X	
	Madden J.W.	X	X	
	Marcus J.	X	X	
	Morwick H.	X	X	
	Peterson J.C.R.	X	X	
	Poole R.B.	X	X	
	Smith A.W.	X	X	
	Taylor E.	X	X	
	Taylor W.	X	X	
	Watson J.	X	X	
	Young A.	X	X	

WAVELLS COLUMN.

		Ba	Tr	Be
Colonel.	Wavell A.G.	X	X	
Capt. S.O.	De Burgh W.J.R.	X	X	

WEBSTERS ROVERS.

		Ba	Tr	Be
Capt.	Webster J.G.		X	
Lt.	Mallett C.M.		X	
Qms.	Bestall C.E.S.			X

WEBSTERS ROVERS.

Rank	Name	Ba	Tr	Be
Pte.	Berry H.		X	
	Darke T.	X	X	
	Green S.		X	
Tpr.	Hartley G.		X	
	Morgan W.S.		X	
Pte.	Scott R.S.		X	
	Wakeford W.J.		X	

WESTERN LEVIES.

Rank	Name	Ba	Tr	Be
Commandant.				
	Mc Taggart H.E.	X	X	
Lt.	Norton J.A.	X	X	
	Venn W.	X	X	
	Vercueil J.M.S.	X	X	

WESTERN RIFLES.

Rank	Name	Ba	Tr	Be
Pte.	Meeser N.			X

WILLOUGHBY'S HORSE.

Rank	Name	Ba	Tr	Be
Capt.	Mc Donald W.D.	X	X	
Lt.	Eastwood E.	X	X	
	Hamilton H.R.	X		
	Henry R.W.	X	X	
Sgt./Maj.	Harris W.	X	X	
Sgt.	Dunsterville A.F.S.	X	X	
	Culpin J.	X	X	
	Hardman A.J.	X		
	Howick G.	X	X	
	Steer T.B.	X		
Cpl.	Glencross R.H.	X	X	
	Prescott B.	X	X	
Pte.	Anderson H.M.	X	X	
Tpr.	Ansell F.W.	X	X	
Pte.	Bonham H.	X	X	
Tpr.	Brailsford W.	X	X	
	Brittain J.D.	X		

WILLOUGHBY'S HORSE contd.

Rank	Name	Ba	Tr	Be
Tpr.	Clark W.	X	X	
	Coburn W.B.	X	X	
	Cunnah T.	X	X	
	Du Plan S.M.	X	X	
	Green E.C.	X	X	
	Gudgeon C.J.	X	X	
	Halforty C.P.	X		
	Hamilton J.	X		
	Hawkins A.C.	X	X	
Pte.	Jenner E.F.	X	X	
Tpr.	Mann C.H.	X	X	
	Marsh C.	X	X	
Pte.	O'Connor P.	X	X	
Tpr.	Ross J.G.	X	X	
	Simpson F.	X	X	
	Solomon S.		X	
	Stewart H.	X		
Pte.	Tatham F.S.	X		
Tpr.	Taylor J.B.	X	X	
	Tooley J.	X		
	Walters C.	X	X	
	Warner H.G.	X	X	
	Wilson L.J.	X	X	

WILLOWMORE BURGHERS.

Rank	Name	Ba	Tr	Be
Capt.	Buckley J.F.	X	X	

WILLOWVALE NATIVE CONTINGENT.

Rank	Name	Ba	Tr	Be
Sgt.	Dingana			X
	Mazamisa W.			X
	Nouma C.			X

WINTERBERG GREYS.

Rank	Name	Ba	Tr	Be
Lt.	Sweetham J.A.	X		
Sgt./Maj.	Sweetham A.G.	X		
Cpl.	Holmes A.	X		
	Timms H.	X		
Tpr.	Bishop W.	X	X	
	Botha T.	X		
	Boucher J.	X		

WINTERBERG GREYS. contd.

Rank	Name	Ba	Tr	Be
Tpr.	Erasmus A.	X		
	Scrooby P.	X		
	Scrooby W.	X		
	Staples J.E.	X	X	
	Staples S.B.	X	X	
	Sweetnam C.F.	X		
	Sweetnam I.H.	X		
	Sweetnam J.J.	X		
	Timms J.	X		

WODEHOUSE BORDER RANGERS. Also listed as WODEHOUSE ROVERS. WODEHOUSE BORDER ROVERS. WODEHOUSE BORDER GUARD.

Rank	Name	Ba	Tr	Be
Capt.	Hulley S.I.		X	
	Hutcheons A.N.M.	X	X	X
	Muhlenbeck F.A.		X	
	Stanford W.E.M.		X	
	Woder C.C.		X	X
Surgeon.	Stanley W.	X	X	
Lt.	Anderson J.D.		X	
Sgt./Maj.	Kuhn C.		X	
Sgt.	Hadley J.T.	X	X	
	Holland D.		X	
	Howett A.C.		X	
	Willard F.		X	
Cpl.	Mulligan J.		X	
	Sutherland A.		X	
Tpr.	Halse C.W.		X	X
	Kuhn F.G.		X	X
	Moore J.		X	
	Sutherland G.		X	

WORCESTER BURGHERS. Also listed as WORCESTER CORPS.

Rank	Name	Ba	Tr	Be
Lt.	Meiring H.C.		X	
Qms.	De Jongh J.N.		X	

WORCESTER BURGHERS. Also listed as WORCESTER CORPS. Contd.

Rank	Name	Ba	Tr	Be
Sgt.	Kloppers J.S.		X	
Cpl.	Meiring P.		X	
Pte.	Adams J.H.		X	
	Butler J.		X	
	du Toit J.J.		X	
	Kirsbaum C.A.		X	
	Mc Laren P.		X	
	Naude A.H.		X	
	Palm R.J.		X	
	Quinn A.C.		X	
	Thorne J.		X	
	Viljoen G.P.		X	

SUNDRY RECIPIENTS.

Secretary for Defence.

Rank	Name	Ba	Tr	Be
Col.	Homan-ffolliott P.			X

Commandant General.

Rank	Name	Ba	Tr	Be
Gen.	Clarke C.M.	X	X	

Commandant Basutoland

	Name	Ba	Tr	Be
	Davies H.L.	X		

Commandant Vol. & Nat. Levies. Transkei

	Name	Ba	Tr	Be
	Elliott H.J.		X	

Commandant.

	Name	Ba	Tr	Be
	Jenner H.A.			X

Staff Officers.

Rank	Name	Ba	Tr	Be
Capt.	Brownlee W.T.		X	

(Also listed as Capt. W. Thompson)

Rank	Name	Ba	Tr	Be
Capt.	Lang E.	X	X	
	Rein A.		X	

SUNDRY RECIPIENTS. Contd.

COLONIAL ARTILLERY.

	Clasps		
	Ba	Tr	Be
Lt.Col. Taylor W.H.F.			X

STAFF.

Interpreter.

	Ba	Tr	Be
Mc Carthy J.P.			X
Qms. Goldsmith L.	X	X	
Lester L.G.	X	X	
Tpr. Louw H.S.J.	X		

No Rank.

	Ba	Tr	Be
Player F.W.	X		

Servant to Maj. Gen. Carrington

	Ba	Tr	Be
Fraser (No Rank or initial)	X		

CHAPLAINS.

	Ba	Tr	Be
Stenson J.W. (Also shown with Stockenstroom Contingent.)	X		
Widdicombe J.	X		

MEDICAL STAFF.

BASE HOSPITAL UMTATA.

Surgeon.

	Ba	Tr	Be
Craister T.L.		X	

Medical Officer.

	Ba	Tr	Be
Addison W.H.		X	
Taylor H.S.	X		

Hospital.

	Ba	Tr	Be
Sgt. Jensen A.J.	X	X	
Hine E.R.	X		
Nurse. Rogers G.A.	No clasps		
Sgt. Schneider A.K.F.	X		

SUNDRY RECIPIENTS. Contd.

INSPECTOR OF TELEGRAPHS

	Clasps		
	Ba	Tr	Be
Smith J.F.		X	

COMMANDEERING FORCE.

	Ba	Tr	Be
No Rank. Hobson G.R.	X		

INDEX

	PAGE
ACKNOWLEDGEMENTS AND THANKS	9
AUTHOR'S NOTES	2, 6
REGULATIONS GOVERNING THE AWARD OF THE MEDAL	5
NO CLASP MEDALS	6
DUPLICATED MEDALS	6
MEDAL TO TROOPER P. BROWN GEORGETOWN BURGHERS	1
TRIPLICATED MEDALS	6
LETTER FROM COMMISSIONER OF POLICE D. 1	23
LIST OF RECIPIENTS OF THE MEDAL WITH THREE CLASPS	7
TOTAL CLASPS - DETAILS	8
TOTAL OF TWO CLASP MEDALS	8
SUNDRY RECIPIENTS OF THE MEDAL	78

A.

ABALONDOLOZI REGIMENT	10
ADELAIDE MOUNTED INFANTRY	10
ADELAIDE MOUNTED IN. VOL.	10
ADELAIDE VOLUNTEERS	10
ALBANY RANGERS	10
ALBERT BURGHERS	10
ALEXANDRIA BURGHERS	10
ALEXANDRIA CONTINGENT	10
ALIWAL NORTH CONTINGENT	11
ALIWAL NORTH VOLUNTEERS	11
AMATEMBU REGIMENT	11
ARMY ORDNANCE CORPS	11

B.

BACA CONTINGENT	11
BAKERS HORSE	11
BARKLEY'S NATIVE CONTING.	12

B. Contd.

	PAGE
BARKLY VOLUNTEERS	12
BASUTO LEVY	12
BASUTOLAND MOUNTED POLICE	12
BASUTO NATIVE CONTINGENT	12
BASUTO NATIVE LEVY	12
BASUTO POLICE	12
BASUTO SPECIAL POLICE	12
BEAUFORT RANGERS	12
BEAUFORT WEST BURGHERS	12
BEAUFORT WEST RIFLES	12
BEAUFORT WEST VOLUNTEER RIFLES	12
BECHUANA F.F.	12
BECHUANALAND FIELD FORCE	12
BECH. S. POLICE	12
BEDFORD BURGHERS	13
BORDER POLICE	13
BREDASDORP BURGHERS	13
BUFF MTD. RANGERS	13
BUFFALO M. VOL.	13
BUFFALO MOUNTED VOLUNTEERS	13
BUFFALO RANGERS	13
BUFFALO VOL.	13
BUFFALO VOL. RIFLES	13
BULLERS MOUNTED	13
BURGHERSDORP BURGHER F.	13
BURGHERS.P VOL.	13

C.

CALEDON BURGHERS	13
CAPE FIELD ARTILLERY	14
CAPE INFANTRY	14
CAPE MEDICAL STAFF CORPS.	14
CAPE M.S. CORPS	14
CAPE MOUNTED RIFLEMAN	14
CAPE MOUNTED YEOMANRY	19

	PAGE
C. contd.	
C.M. YEO	19
CAPE POLICE DISTRICT No. 1	24
CAPE POLICE DISTRICT No. 2	30
CAPE POLICE	32
CAPE TOWN HIGHLANDERS	33
CAPE TOWN RANGERS	34
CAPE TOWN RIFLES	35
CAPE TOWN VOLUNTEER ARTILLERY	36
CAPE TOWN VOLUNTEER ENGINEERS	36
CAPE YEOMANRY	19
CATHCART BURGHERS	36
CERES BURGHERS	37
CHALUMNA MOUNTED VOLUNTEERS	37
CHALUMNA VOL.	37
CHALUMNA VOL. CAVALRY	37
COLESBERG BURGHERS	37
COLESBURG VOLS.	37
COLONIAL FORCES	37
COMMANDANT GENERAL'S STAFF	37
COMMISSARIAT DEPT.	37
COMM. & TRANSPORT	37
CRADOCK BURGHERS	38
CRADOCK INFANTRY	38
CRADOCK VOLUNTEERS	38
CRADOCK VOLUNTEER RIFLES	38
D.	
DENNISONS HORSE	38
DESPATCH RIDER	38
DIAMOND FIELDS ARTILLERY	38
DIAMOND FIELDS HORSE	39
DICKS KAFFRARIAN LEVIES	40
DICKS LEVIES	40
DICKS NATIVE LEVIES	40
DIMES RIFLES	45

	PAGE
D. contd.	
DUKE OF EDINBURGH OWN VOL. RIFLES	41
DYMES RIFLES	45
E.	
EAST GRIQUALAND FORCES	46
EAST LONDON ARTILLERY	46
E. LONDON VOLS.	46
EAST LONDON VOLUNTEER INFANTRY	46
F.	
F.A.M. POLICE	48
FERREIRAS HORSE	46
FIELD FORCE	46
FINGO LEVIES	46
FINGO LEVIES KAMASTONE	54
FINGO SCOUTS	46
FINGO VOLUNTEERS	46
FIRST CITY GRAHAMSTOWN VOL.	46
FIRST CITY MOUNTED VOLUNTEERS	46
FIRST CITY VOLUNTEERS	46
FORT BEAUFORT VOLUNTEERS	48
FORT WHITE VOLUNTEERS	48
FRONTIER ARMED & MOUNTED POLICE	48
FRONTIER CARABINEERS	48
FRONTIER CARBINEERS	48
FROSTS COLUMN	48
G.	
GELUK MOUNTED VOLUNTEERS	49
GENERAL CLARKE'S STAFF	49
GENERAL SERVICE	49
GEORGE BURGHERS	49
GEORGETOWN BURGHERS	49
GEORGE VOLUNTEERS	49

	PAGE
G. Contd.	
GNUBIE M. RIFLES	49
GONUBIE HORSE	49
GONUBIE M$^{td.}$ VOL.	49
GORDONIA VOLUNTEERS	49
GRAAFF REINET BURGHERS	50
GRAAFF REINET ROVERS	50
GRAHAMSTOWN MOUNTED INFANTRY	50
GRAHAMSTOWN HORSE ARTY	50
GRAHAMSTOWN VOL. H. ARTILLERY	50
GRAYS GONUBIE VOLUNTEERS	51
GRAYS G.M. VOLS.	51
GRIQUALAND WEST BRIGADE	51
GRIQUALAND WEST NATIVE CONTG.	51
H.	
HAMPSHIRE ARTILLERY	51
HARVEYS HORSE	52
HELVENS HORSE	52
HERSCHEL NATIVE CONTINGENT	52
HOPETOWN BURGHERS	52
HUMANSDORP BURGHERS	52
HUMANSDORP LIGHT HORSE	52
HUMANSDORP VOLUNTEERS	52
HUNTS VOLUNTEERS	52
I.	
IDUTYWA LEVIES	52
IDUTYWA MILITIA	52
INTELLIGENCE	52
IRREGULAR HORSE	52
J.	
JAMESTOWN VOLUNTEERS	52

	PAGE
K.	
KAFFRARIAN LEVIES	52
KAFFRARIAN RIFLES	53
KAFFRARIAN VOLUNTEER ARTILLERY	54
KAMATONE FINGOS	54
KAMASTONE LEVY	54
KEISKAMA HOEK VOLUNTEERS	54
KIMBERLEY HORSE	54
KIMBERLEY LIGHT HORSE	54
KIMBERLEY REGIMENT	55
KIMBERLEY REG. - VOL.s	55
KIMBERLEY RIFLES	55
KINGS ROYAL RIFLES THE 3rd	57
KING WILLIAMS TOWN VOL. ARTILLERY	57
KNYSNA VOLUNTEERS	57
KOKSTAD MOUNTED RIFLES	57
KOKSTAD MOUNTED VOLUNTEERS	57
KOMGHA BURGHERS	58
KOMGHA MOUNTED VOLUNTEERS	58
L.	
LADY FRERE NATIVE LEVY	58
LADY FRERE LEVY	58
LANDREYS HORSE	58
LANDREYS LIGHT HORSE	58
LEACHES RIFLES	59
LEARYS NATIVE LEVIES	59
LERIBE LEVY	59
LERIBE NATIVE LEVY	59
LONSDALE RIFLES	59
M.	
MACLEAR CONSTAB.	59
MACLEAR SPL. CONS.	59

	PAGE
M. contd.	
MACLEAR NAT. LEVIES	59
MAFEKING MOUNTED RIFLES	59
MAFETENG CONTINGENT	59
MAFETENG NATIVE CONT.	59
MAFETENG VOLS.	59
MALMESBURY BURGHERS	60
MALMESBURY LEVIES	60
MASERU NATIVE LEVIES	60
MASERU VOLUNTEERS	60
McNICHOLAS HORSE	60
MIDDELBURG BURGHERS	60
MAHALES HOEK CONTG.	60
MEDICAL STAFF	79
MOHALI HOEK CONTINGENT	60
MOUNT AYLIFF VOL.	60
MOUNT TEMPLE HORSE	60
MURRAYSBURG BURGHERS	60
MUTERS RANGERS	60
N.	
NATAL CONSTABULARY	60
NATAL MOUNTED POLICE	60
NATAL MOUNTED RIFLES	61
NATIVE BASUTO LEVY	61
NATIVE CONTINGENT	61
NATIVE CONTINGENT TEMBULAND	61
NATIVE LEVIES	61
NATIVE POLICE QUITHING CONTG.	70
NESBITTS HORSE	61
NESBITTS LIGHT HORSE	61
NETTLETON IRREGULAR HORSE	52
O.	
ORDNANCE DEPARTMENT	62
OUDTSHOORN BURGHERS	63
OUDTSHOORN VOLUNTEER RIFLES	63

	PAGE
P.	
PAARL BURGHERS	64
PAARL WESTERN LEVIES	64
PAPKUIL MOUNTED RIFLE CLUB	64
PAPKUIL RIFLES	64
PORT ELIZABETH RIFLES	64
PRINCE ALBERT BURGHERS	64
P.A.O.C.A.	64
PRINCE ALFREDS OWN CAPE VOL. ARTILLERY	64
PRINCE ALFREDS VOLUNTEER GUARD	65
PULLENS HORSE	68
PULLENS RANGERS	68
Q.	
QUEENSTOWN BURGHERS	68
QUEENSTOWN DIVISION	69
QUEENSTOWN FLYING COL.	69
QUEENSTOWN RIFLE VOLUNTEERS	69
QUEENSTOWN VOL.	68
QUMBU CONTINGENT	70
QUTHENG & MASITISI NATIVE CONTG.	70
R.	
RICHMOND BURGHERS	70
ROSS AND HICKSONS HORSE	70
ROSS' HORSE	70
ROSS' LIGHT HORSE	70
ROYAL IRISH FUSILEERS 3RD	70
S.	
SALEM RANGERS	70
SCHERMANS BURGHERS	70
SCOUTS	70
SEVENTH HUSSARS	70
SIXTIETH RIFLES - 3RD	70
SOMERSET EAST BURGHERS	71
SOMERSET EAST CONT.	71

	PAGE		PAGE
S. contd.		**T. contd.**	
SOUTHEYVILLE LEVIES	71	THOMPSON RELIEF COLUMN	73
SPECIAL BORDER POLICE	71	TRANS M.R.	73
STANFORDS POLICE	71	TRANSKEI FINGO MILITIA	73
STANFORDS SPECIAL POLICE	71	TRANSKEI NATIVE CONTINGENT	73
STANTONS HORSE	71	TRANSKEI NATIVE LEVIES	73
STANTONS LIGHT HORSE	71	TRANSKEI NATIVE MILITIA	73
STAFF OF GENERAL CLARKE	49	TRANSPORT CORPS	73
STELLALAND HORSE	71	TRANSVAAL HORSE	74
STELLALAND LIGHT HORSE	71	TRUE BLUES	74
STELLENBOSCH BURGHERS	72	TSOLO NAT. CONTG.	74
STERKSTROOM RIFLES	72	TSOLO NAT. LEVIES	74
STOCKENSTROOM BURGHERS	72	TSOLO NAT. MILITIA	74
STOCKENSTROOM CONTG.	72		
STOCKENSTROOM HOTT. CONTG.	72		
STOCKENSTROOM LEVIES	72	**U.**	
STOCKENSTROOM RANGERS	72		
STOCKENSTROOM VOLS.	72	UITENHAGE BURGHERS	74
STOCKENSTROOM VOL. RIFLES	72	UMTATA MOUNTED VOLUNTEERS	75
STRACHANS NATIVE CONTG.	72	UMTATA NATIVE CONTINGENT	75
STRACHANS NAT. LEVIES	72	UMTATA VOLUNTEERS	75
STUTTERHEIM L.I. VOLS.	72	UPINGTON SPECIAL POLICE	75
STUTTERHEIM VOLS.	72	USHERS CONTINGENT	75
SWELLENDAM BURGHERS	72	USHERS RANGERS	75
T.		**V.**	
TAMBOOKIE WARD BURGHERS	72	VIC RNGS. M^{td} POLICE	75
TARKA. B	72	VICTORIA RANGERS	75
TARKA VOLUNTEER RIFLES	73	VICTORIAN RANGERS	75
TARKASTAD BURGHERS	72	VICTORIA RIFLES	75
TAUNGS GUN DETACHMENT	73	VICTORIA WEST RANGERS	75
TELEGRAPHIC & INTELLIGENCE STAFF	73	VOLUNTEER MEDICAL STAFF CORPS	75
TEMBULAND F.F.	73	V. MEDICAL STAFF CORPS	75
TEMBU LEVIES	73	V.M.S.C.	75
THIRD ROYAL IRISH RIFLES	70	VRYBURG BURGHERS	76

PAGE

V. contd.

VRYBURG MOUNTED VOLUNTEERS	76
VRYBURG VOLUNTEERS	76

W.

WALKERS RIFLES	76
WAVELLS COLUMN	76
WEBSTERS ROVERS	76
WESTERN LEVIES	77
WESTERN RIFLES	77
WILLOUGHBY'S HORSE	77
WILLOWMORE BURGHERS	77
WILLOWVALE NATIVE CONTINGENT	77
WINTERBERG GREYS	77
WODEHOUSE BORDER GUARD	78
WODEHOUSE BORDER RANGERS	78
WODEHOUSE BORDER ROVERS	78
WODEHOUSE ROVERS	78
WORCESTER BURGHERS	78
WORCESTER CORPS.	78